How to Build Fences, Gates, and Walls

How to

Build Fences, Gates, and Walls

by Stanley Schuler

Collier Books

A Division of Macmillan Publishing Co., Inc.

New York

Collier Macmillan Publishers

London

Macmillan Publishing Co., Inc.
866 Third Avenue, New York, N.Y. 10022
Collier Macmillan Canada, Ltd.

Library of Congress Cataloging in Publication Data
Schuler, Stanley.
How to build fences, gates, and walls.
Includes index.
1. Fences. 2. Gates. 3. Walls. I. Title.
TH4965.S37   1976b   717   75-35662
ISBN 0-02-000840-6

How to Build Fences, Gates, and Walls is also published
in a hardcover edition by Macmillan Publishing Co., Inc.

All photographs by the author except as noted.
Some of them appear in an earlier book, *America's
Great Private Gardens*.

First Collier Books Edition 1976

Printed in the United States of America

Contents

How to Build Fences, Gates, and Walls

1 Choosing the Right Barrier for Your Purpose

No one knows when man built his first wall. It was probably while he was still a savage. He just rolled rocks into a pile large enough to slow a marauding beast while he pelted it with stones.

Fences probably came along at about the same time. They were built by men living in forests rather than on the plains. They had no more style than the early walls; were made simply of fallen trees piled into a confused mass.

When man started to build walls and fences to a definite thought-out design is also lost in the mists of time; but it must have been many centuries later, when cities started to spring up. One of the earliest walls mentioned by historians is the famous one that protected Jericho until Joshua came along somewhere about 1200 BC. Another was the huge wall surrounding Troy until the Greeks breeched it with a wooden horse about 500 BC. Still younger is the Great Wall of China, on which work started about 200 BC. It has the distinction of being one of the few early walls still standing.

My only reason for touching on the history of walls is to emphasize the important role they have played for so many thousands of years. Today, walls are more important than ever. True, we haven't counted on them very much to save lives since Hitler made a mockery of the walls and bunkers of the Maginot Line. But think for a moment of the many reasons why the modern homeowner builds walls and fences:

- To discourage or actually keep out trespassers—both human and animal.

- To keep people from seeing into the house, terrace, and/or yard.

- To reduce street noises and dirt in the house.

- To prevent children and pets from drowning in swimming pools. (This is the only case in which there are laws requiring homeowners to build fences or walls.)

- To keep sloping land from sliding and/or to provide flat spaces for gardening, games, etc., on hillside lots.

1

- To stop children, pets, and livestock from straying.

- To delineate property boundaries and areas within the property.

- To serve as a background for plants.

- To keep neighbors from annoying one another.

- To conceal unattractive sights such as garage turnarounds, compost heaps, and garbage cans.

- To ward off winds battering terraces, play areas, etc.

- To stop snow from drifting.

In the historic section of Ste. Genevieve, Missouri, almost every property is surrounded by a fence. One can imagine that an itinerant Tom Sawyer had a hand in painting this plain board fence.

This is indeed an era of fences and walls. And in one way that is unfortunate because so many of these barriers are necessitated by our efforts to protect ourselves from the deleterious by-products of mushrooming growth. As a result, a high percentage of new walls and fences are strictly functional—and ugly. One of the sorriest things that ever happened to our magnificent country was the invention of chain-link fencing.

On the other hand, the proliferating need for fences and walls can be considered a boon because we are given that many more opportunities to beautify our properties with them. I really mean this: If well designed and well constructed, fences and walls are

2

not only charming in themselves but also contribute, often significantly, to the beauty of the grounds on which they stand.

The great majority of the walls and fences I have used for illustrations prove this. Some, of course, have much more impact than others (a few are included simply because they are good utility fences). But even the solid-board fence on the opposite page proves the point. I won't go so far as to say the fence itself is beautiful (though it most certainly is not homely). But it definitely makes a contribution to the appearance of the property. For one thing, it imparts an air of mystery to the yard and garden area we cannot see; and in this sort of situation, we tend to glamorize mystery and consequently imagine the yard to be prettier than it may actually be. For another thing, the fence extends the lines of the house and makes it appear larger and more welcoming. At the same time, the fence helps to enhance the appearance of the house by drawing the eye down away from the maze of utility wires that desecrate the sky and spoil the lines of the roof.

The interesting thing is that I don't believe the fence was intended to do any of these things. The house is in the ancient Mississippi River town of Ste. Genevieve, Missouri; and from its beginning days, the residents of Ste. Genevieve made a practice of surrounding their houses and yards with stockade fences to fend off Indians. Most of the old properties are still fenced (though usually not with stockade fences)—probably just out of habit.

But the old-timers had a facility for investing even such a simple, essentially utilitarian thing as a fence or wall with beauty; and if there is one thing this book does, I hope it helps to transmit some of this former feeling for fences and walls to the current generation. No matter how prosaic their purpose, there is no reason under the sun why fences and walls around and in residential properties must be as dull and unsightly as the chain-link design which is so widely used. This is not to say that they should be as elaborate as, say, the fences on pages 5, 24, and 25. Such structures today would cost a great deal. But if you need a fence or wall, your money is far better spent if you try to make it attractive as well as useful.

One of the more depressing trips I have made in recent years was to Carmel, California. Carmel is a charming town. People come every weekend from miles around to stroll the shady streets lined with beguiling shops, homes, and gardens. But the fences were to me utterly depressing (and at that time, I hadn't the faintest idea I would ever write a book about such things, so I wasn't predisposed to give them much attention).

Carmel homeowners need fences and walls (there are not many of the latter) to keep the milling throngs out of their gardens. And I must say that the appearance of the fences is in part attributable to these throngs, who lean on them, shove them, and strike them with their cars. But the fences were obviously a drab lot to start with and poorly constructed (which is another reason why visitors have such an easy time maltreating them).

By contrast, the village of Nantucket, Massachusetts, which is also overrun with visitors, boasts one of the handsomest collections of fences and walls (again, there are not many walls) I have ever seen. Many, to be sure, are very old and display that beauty and solidity that are the hallmarks of old fences. But the new ones are attractive, too. All add immeasurably to the charm of the town; and I daresay that many tourists ferrying back to Woods Hole find themselves remarking about them.

I have no intention of speculating on why two similar communities have such divergent views about fences and walls. Neither, to digress somewhat, shall I speculate on why Louisville, Kentucky, has a dearth of fences and walls—good or bad—while the similar city of Memphis, Tennessee, is overloaded with them—mostly good. These are questions for sociologists to answer.

My only point, which I have belabored just about enough, is that walls and fences can be beautiful. And they should be.

But obviously you feel the same way, otherwise you wouldn't be reading this book.

I'll get further into the business of how to make them beautiful in later chapters. The question right now concerns more practical matters:

What kind of fence or wall do you need around your home?

(Opposite) A work of art—perfect in every detail. Yet when you analyze the fence, you discover that it is quite simple and, except for the pineapple finials on the gate posts, would not be difficult to copy.

Both kinds of barriers serve essentially the same purposes. By and large, they are interchangeable. In fact, both were called fences in the early days of our country (and even today, both are lumped under the word "fences" in state and municipal statutes). Those built of wood were called fences, and those built of stone, the other common building material, were called stone fences. Today, needless to say, we make a distinction between them. Walls are built of

4

masonry; fences of wood, plywood, hardboard, plastics, asbestos-cement board, glass—everything except masonry.

Fences and walls compete with hedges for the right to divide and protect properties. Hedges have several advantages: They blend into the landscape and can be as formal, informal, or naturalistic as you like. They give better protection against wind. And if you start with small plants, they cost less initially as well as in the long run.

Fences take up less space than either walls or hedges. They are more quickly constructed and give you almost instantaneously whatever results you expect from them. There is practically no limit to the ways in which they can be designed. They cost less than walls and require less maintenance than hedges. But they eventually have to be replaced in whole or in part.

Walls are intermediate between fences and hedges in the amount of space they require and in the speed with which they attain full size. But they take top honors in durability, ease of maintenance, and rugged beauty. On the other hand, they come in a sorry last in the cost competition.

Which of the three barriers is the hardest to get past—either by going over it, through it, or under it—is a toss up. Walls are generally thought to give the best protection against automobiles, trucks, and other types of battering rams; but steel fencing is used along the nation's highways because it's just as tough and costs much less. Dense hedges of rambler roses have also proved excellent.

If the aim is to hold people at bay, a sturdy fence is just about as effective as a wall; and neither has any advantage over a dense hedge—especially if it is armed with thorns or prickly leaves.

Similarly, if you want to keep people from climbing over the top of a barrier, fences are no more effective than walls and both are inferior to hedges, which would collapse under the weight of anyone foolish enough to make the attempt.

The only clear point of superiority which fences and walls enjoy over hedges when it comes to stopping intruders is their psychological value. They say "keep out" louder and more authoritatively. I am not altogether sure why this is, but it's probably because we share early man's feeling that fences and walls are meant primarily for protection whereas hedges, no matter how impenetrable they may be, are simply screens or dividers. Or perhaps it's because

6

High, white-painted brick wall and high black gate clearly say "keep out." They don't even allow peeking. The wall is capped with slabs of stone like those on which it stands.

hedges, being made of plants, look like part of the landscape whereas walls and fences are alien to it and seem uncordial as a result.

Psychology plays a rather important role in the construction of fences and walls designed to give privacy; and if you don't want to spend more money than necessary, it's a good idea to take this into account when building for this purpose.

To all except the closest friends of the homeowner, any fence or wall which surrounds a house is a warning to keep out. It follows that, if the purpose of a fence or wall is simply to discourage people passing by your house from straying into the yard, a low one is just as effective as a high one. True, there will always be some one— usually a child—who chooses to ignore the warning; but most people will obey. (And most dogs will, too, not because they understand the meaning of fences but because a compelling reason is needed to make them jump over something which is taller than they are.)

A high fence or wall is needed only if the purpose is to keep people from looking into your yard or if there is some reason for emphasizing the fact that trespassers are not welcome. But here we run up against another peculiarity of human nature. To be fully effective in stopping people from peering into a yard, a fence or wall must be not only solid but also high enough so they can't see over it. If it isn't solid, it simply challenges certain people to peer through the openings out of curiosity. Similarly, if it's less than about 5 ft. high, it challenges them to stand on tiptoe and look over the top.

For almost total privacy, a high, solid fence or wall must have an equally high and solid gate. This is a clear indication to the average person that he isn't wanted; and it also gives pause to the brash because they have no way of knowing whether a vicious dog is waiting for them on the other side. By contrast, if a person can see through or over a gate in a solid barrier, he may pause a second

A pleasant relief from the usual chain-link fence used around swimming pools. This 4-ft. fence is made with sharply pointed half logs for pickets. The smooth front of the fence is faced toward the neighboring properties to make it harder to climb.
PHOTO BY MILLARD J. MEYERS FOR PRINCE HILL POOLS

to digest its meaning; but if he sees the coast is clear, he may then push right on through. Another drawback of a see-through-or-over gate is that, like a see-through-or-over fence, it invites people to stop and look in.

Psychology also enters into the fencing of swimming pools. I have long been skeptical of the value of 4-ft. chain-link fences around pools—even though they are endorsed by law enforcers—because I think that, while they may discourage some children, they goad others. Any reasonably athletic youngster can climb a chain-link fence; and when confronted with one around an enticing pool, many feel compelled to do so. A far better barrier is a solid board fence or brick or concrete block wall that doesn't afford a foothold. Equally good—and perhaps better—is a 6-ft. fence or wall with or without footholds because only the most agile and daring youngster has confidence in his ability to scale it.

Psychology plays little if any part in the construction of fences and walls built for other purposes. But there are a good many practical and aesthetic points which should be considered:

Barriers To Keep Children from Straying

The same kinds of fence and wall which will keep children from falling into a pool will keep them from fleeing the property. They must be high and hard to climb.

Barriers To Keep Dogs from Straying

Most people select chain-link fencing for this purpose because it is not worn by scratching, is completely resistant to gnawing and clawing and can be buried and/or embedded in a ribbon of concrete to keep dogs from digging underneath. But in addition to its sad appearance, it has one flaw (which it shares with other types of wire-mesh fencing): Some dogs can climb it like monkeys. I admit the number isn't great; but it isn't insignificant either—and that's a point worth thinking about if you really value your animal or fear for the damage it may do to people or property if it breaks loose. So I recommend that before you cage him up for good, test him in a temporary pen for a week or so.

Barriers To Delineate Boundaries

Any fence or wall will do this. But beware of the very low 12- to 18-in.-high picket fence you often see around garden areas and raised terraces: It's entirely too easy to trip over when you back up against it, chase something across the yard, or wander around in the dark. To prevent such accidents, a fence should not be much less than 27 in. high.

Barriers To Serve As Backgrounds for Plants

Any reasonably solid fence, regardless of height, forms a good background if the plants displayed against it are in scale with it. In other words, a 3-ft. fence can make a good background for a flower bed; but you must be standing fairly close to it to get the full effect. This means that the height of the fence must also be in rough scale with the size of the area enclosed. For example, if you want a background for plants around an entire 100- × 200-ft. lot, a fence 4 to 6 ft. high is called for.

The height of a fence or wall used as a background is just one of several things you should think about. Others are the construction and color of the barrier.

Generally, the best background for plants is one which is fairly smooth and solid (so its texture doesn't compete with the plants) and light in color (preferably white, light gray, or tan because they are neutral in tone and contrast well with plant colors). Happily, there are several kinds of fences and walls which meet these requirements; even so, few make perfect backgrounds. Why? Because whenever you plant close to fences or walls or train plants on them, you create problems.

For example, plants trained on fences are sometimes so heavy

White-painted stone wall curves around garden in a big, slightly imperfect semicircle. English ivy is carefully trained on wires to form an open diamond pattern. The double gate repeats the pattern.

that they bring about the collapse of the fences. This obviously is preventable, but only if you recognize the possible danger before building a fence or selecting plants for it.

Another problem is that, if you train plants on a fence or wall which is painted, you cannot repaint properly unless you take the plants down. This is not too difficult—though it isn't easy, either— if the plants are nonclinging vines which are tied to the fence or wall with strings or wires. But if you prefer clinging plants such as English or Boston ivy or wintercreeper, they should be trained only

A tiny terrace is shielded from a neighboring house only a few feet away by a stockade fence and rolls of woven reeds which are extended over the terrace to keep off the sun.

Lattice fences are good windbreaks and obscure vision without totally cutting it off; but they collect dirt and are hard to paint. In this brand new fence, the lattice strips are nailed to 4 x 4-in. posts and 2 x 4-in. rails; and 6-in. boards are nailed over the edges and joints in the strips.

on unpainted walls or fences, because once they establish themselves, they shouldn't be removed.

A third problem to be considered, if you live in a humid or semihumid climate, is that plants growing close to walls and fences precipitate the growth of algae on the surfaces they shade. This, in turn, causes large spreading stains, ruins paint, and leads to the decay of wood. Furthermore, removal of the algae can be accomplished only by thorough, hard scrubbing with a strong chlorine solution which may splatter on and damage the plants creating the problem in the first place.

Barriers To Keep Neighbors from Annoying One Another

The only completely satisfactory barrier for this purpose is a high, unbroken fence or wall which is capable not only of blocking sight and the passage of people, dogs, and balls but also of muffling sounds. In addition, the fence builder must weigh the impact that the appearance of the fence or wall will have on the neighbor; but I'll talk about this in the next chapter.

Barriers To Conceal Unattractive Sights

These should be high enough so you can't see what is behind them from any point where you're likely to be sitting or standing. They don't always have to form a solid curtain, however, because unless the area behind the barrier is bathed in sunlight, a semiopen fence or wall obstructs the view quite adequately.

A semiopen barrier is, in fact, much better than a solid one if used to conceal a garage turnaround or parking area because a viewer is aware when a car is moving and the driver is aware of the viewer. Thus both persons are more or less on the alert for whomever suddenly emerges from behind the barrier.

Barriers To Ward Off Winds

Very few people understand that a solid fence or wall is not a good wind barrier unless the area is roofed; and in that case, the fence is a building wall and not the kind of free-standing wall which this book is about.

To protect terrace from winds driving off the Pacific Ocean while retaining a view of the ocean, a high screen of plate glass was built around the windward sides. The glass is laid up against the outer edges of the posts and rails and is held in place by boards. Normally, glass panels are surrounded by the posts and rails.

Suppose you have a terrace which is buffeted by a seabreeze. To get relief, you build a 6-ft. solid-board fence along the ocean side of the terrace. Much to your chagrin, however, you will find that the only quiet area on the terrace is in the immediate lee of the fence. When you're sitting on the opposite side of the terrace, the breeze is about as annoying as ever.

The explanation is quite simple. Wind, in effect, has eyes. As it whistles across the land, it sees the high fence in its way and, just before reaching the fence, vaults over it, comes down on the other side and keeps on going. It is like a man running a 110-meter high-hurdle race.

Three pictures of an extraordinarily handsome solid-board fence. About 8 ft. high, it completely surrounds the front and side yards of a home at the corner of two city streets which roar with traffic twenty-four hours a day. Thus it protects the first floor of the house against the noise and at the same time affords almost total privacy when the owners are outdoors. The beauty of the gray-stained fence stems from the frequent deep jogs, which produce a rare texture and shadow pattern. Without these, the fence would look like a forbidding prison wall.

Now, suppose you rebuild the fence with boards spaced about an inch apart or with latticework, louvers, or some other type of openwork. Suddenly, your terrace is no longer buffeted by wind. What has happened is that the wind, approaching the fence, sees it isn't solid; so it tries to whistle right on through the openings. But just as a colander breaks up and slows a stream of water, the openings in the fence break up and dissipate the wind; and what emerges on the lee side is reduced to a zephyr.

A semiopen fence or wall, in other words, is usually the best protection against wind. It's only when you have a precious view that you should use a solid barrier—of glass or plastic.

Barriers To Stop Noise

When I was looking for fences and walls to photograph for this book, one of the most productive areas I found was in Cambridge, Massachusetts, near where Mount Auburn Street crosses Fresh Pond Parkway. Many of the fences (there are very few walls) were as old and beautifully detailed as the houses they graced (in fact, one of them, shown on page 5, was the loveliest fence I think I have seen anywhere). But many others were modern and tall—erected, obviously, to minimize the steady rumble of traffic on the thoroughfares.

More and more people in all parts of the country are being forced to build walls and fences for the same reason. In fact, the problem of highway noise has become so acute that the U.S. Department of Housing and Urban Development recently commissioned Bolt, Beranek, and Newman, the eminent Waltham, Massachusetts, acoustical engineering firm, to prepare recommendations for how to cope with it.

I, too, have questioned BB&N, and from what I was told, it is patently clear that noise control is one of the major contributions that walls and fences can make to today's homeowners. Hedges, despite some opinion to the contrary, are of no value. As Robert Newman says, "They provide only a visual barrier—out of sight, out of mind."

To be effective as noise barriers, however, walls and fences must be properly designed and built.

1. Above all else, they must be as high as possible. To quote Mr. Newman: "A wall (or fence) that does not cut off line-of-sight between the listener and the source of noise does absolutely nothing. A 10-ft.-high brick wall in front of a six-story apartment

building provides no benefit at all for the people on upper floors who can look down and see the cars. But it may help the person on the ground floor as long as it cuts off his line-of-sight to the traffic."

Conclusion: If you live on a flat lot level with a busy street used only by automobiles and pickup trucks, a 4- to 6-ft. fence will do a good job of protecting garden and first floor from the noise of traffic; but it will probably be inadequate at the second-floor level. If your lot and house are below street level, a lower fence will do the trick. On the other hand, if your lot slopes up from the street, the fence must be much taller.

If traffic on your street includes big trucks—especially highway behemoths—the fence in all cases must be much, much higher so you can't see—and hear—the truck engines.

2. The wall or fence should either extend as far as possible in both directions along the street or be wrapped around your lot so passing automobiles are hidden from view at all points.

If the fence is interrupted for a front walk or driveway, the opening either must be closed with a gate or a protective panel that is built a few feet back from the opening and overlapping it.

3. The wall or fence must be of solid, fairly weighty material such as wood, plywood, asbestos-cement board, plastic, glass, metal, brick, or concrete. Equally important, it must be airtight, because if air can pass through it, noise can, too. This doesn't mean that joints must be caulked, but they must be close fitting. In addition, the bottom of the fence must be tight to the ground.

4. The wall or fence must be built either close to the street or close to the house or garden area which you want to shield. A wall that is halfway between the house and street is less effective.

5. Vines on the wall should not be allowed to extend above the top because they interfere with the passage of sound and deflect some of it downward. Tall trees close to the wall on either side should be avoided for the same reason.

2 Laws and Keeping Neighbors Happy

The first American fence laws were passed in Virginia in 1632. They required farmers to erect fences to protect their crops. The other colonies soon followed suit.

For example, in 1643, the ruling court in Connecticut noted that if something were not done to improve the fences in various communities in order to keep cattle from ruining crops, the public peace might be prejudiced. Thirty years later the court decreed that every landowner must make and maintain "sufficient" fences around his fields, otherwise he would have no recourse against the owner of well-behaved animals that got into the fields. To put teeth into this law, the court also required each town to appoint fence viewers to inspect all fences twice a year. The viewers had authority to order improvements made in any fence found insufficient; and if the owner didn't take action promptly, the viewers were supposed to do the work themselves and charge the owners double recompense.

Today, laws requiring construction of fences or walls are generally limited to farmers and people owning swimming pools. As noted in the preceding chapter, most communities throughout the country require all pools to be surrounded by nonclimbable fences at least 4 ft. high. In some places, the law is extended to require fencing around any kind of pond a person may put in. And if you were to dig a quarry, you would have to fence that also.

Most modern written and unwritten regulations about fences, however, are more concerned with what you should not do than with what you should do.

Fence Height   The height of fences and walls is regulated in some communities and not in others. Generally, anything up to 4 ft. is permissible everywhere. But if you want to go higher than this, you should check your town ordinances to make sure it's legal. Many communities allow 6-ft. fences; some allow 8. But in both cases, the fences may not be permitted in the front yard—only around the backyard.

Fence Sufficiency

"Sufficient" is a word used in legal circles to describe a fence which is capable of keeping cattle and other large animals off a property. If you have a sufficient fence around your property and animals somehow get through, the owner of the animals is considered to be at fault and is required to pay for damage done by the creatures. On the other hand, if animals enter a property with an insufficient fence, the property owner has only himself to blame.

Laws regarding human beings who trespass on property are construed and enforced in so many different ways by U.S. courts that the sufficiency or insufficiency of a fence may not mean very much. But it is fairly safe to say that if you surrounded your yard with a fence sufficient to keep out most people and animals, you would have a better chance defending yourself against a lawsuit brought by a person who trespassed on the property and broke his leg than if the fence were insufficient.

So what constitutes a sufficient fence?

Requirements vary with the community or state, but in all cases the fences must be 4 to 4½ ft. high and constructed of sturdy, hard-to-climb materials.

Fences Bordering Streets and Highways

Fences and walls which block the view of drivers on streets and highways are obviously dangerous and therefore prohibited by the building codes of many communities. The critical areas are at corners and sharp bends in streets. As a rule, no fence more than 3 ft. high can be erected in such locations. Higher fences and walls must be set well back from the street (the exact distance depends on the code).

This high, white fence is set far enough back from the street so cars can enter and leave the driveway safely. The fence looks like a horizontal board-and-board fence, but the back is actually covered with solid panels of plywood. This creates a marvelous shadow-box effect when the sun is overhead.

An attractive, different, and easy-to-build fence that is identical on front and back. It consists of wide rough-sawn cedar boards alternating with slender cedar saplings. Boards and saplings are set loose between the top and bottom rails and held in place by narrow boards nailed to the rails.

Even along straight stretches of street codes usually stipulate that fences cannot be built at the street line but must be set back of the sidewalk or strip of land on which a sidewalk might some day be built.

High fences at the intersections of driveways and streets are not regulated. Ordinary common sense should, however, dictate that all solid fences built in these locations must be angled or rounded so drivers have a clear view of the street as they leave a driveway and an equally clear view of the driveway as they turn in from the street.

Another unregulated matter is the color of fences and walls bordering streets. This is something to worry about if a barrier is placed so that it reflects the light of the late afternoon sun into the eyes of on-coming drivers. In that case, it should not be painted white or be made of a highly reflective material such as glass or shiny plastic.

Division Fences

A division fence or wall separates one property from another. It is the subject of more legal battles than any other kind of fence.

In the United States, any property owner can erect a fence or wall squarely on his boundary, or division, line at his own expense as long as there are no deed restrictions or covenants prohibiting it and as long as the neighbor on the other side agrees to it. But once the fence is completed, half of it automatically belongs to the neighbor because half of it is on his side of the boundary line. Right here is where trouble starts.

You may think that because your neighbor is co-owner of the fence he ought now to pay half the cost of its erection and maintenance. But no. In some states (not all), you may be able to extract his share of the building cost by going to the authorities; but there's nothing you can do to force him to pay for maintenance or even to do any maintenance. He can use his side of the fence as he likes; paint it as he likes; let it go to wrack and ruin if he likes. The only thing he is specifically required to do is to refrain from damaging it.

Obviously, this isn't a very good way to build a fence.

If you want to center a division fence on a boundary line, a more sensible approach is to enlist your neighbor's active coopera-

Basket-weave fences look the same front and back and therefore make excellent division fences since your neighbors can't complain you gave them "the bum side to look at." This is an especially handsome fence made of 12-in., brown-stained boards, woven around 4- x 4-in. posts.

tion in the project. This not only cuts your cost but also gives him a positive feeling of ownership and thus—hopefully—inspires him to take care of his side of the fence. However, the arrangement also gives him an equal say in the appearance and construction of the fence. And it does not guarantee that he will sustain interest in maintaining the fence or will continue on friendly terms with you in regard to it.

There is one other problem about centering a fence on a boundary line that can occur whether you pay the entire cost of the fence or split it with your neighbor: If he gets angry with you and refuses to maintain his side, and you walk around the fence to do his work for him, you can be accused of trespassing.

To avoid all these knotty and sometimes nasty problems, many property owners erect division fences as much as 12 to 18 in. within their own borders. True, this reduces the usable area of their lots. On the other hand, it does assure that the fences will be properly maintained and that their owners can build them, paint them, and plant them as they please.

But remember that it does not stop neighbors from resenting the fences and complaining volubly about their appearance. Hence this rule: If you want a pleasant relationship with neighbors, always build a division fence which is as attractive on their side as on yours.

3 Fence Building

With a few minor exceptions, one fence is built very much like another. As a rule, it's not a job you need to turn over to an expert. But it is advisable—though not essential—to have a helper assist in such things as aligning posts and fitting and nailing rails. Above all, you should not hurry your work because the result will be a sloppy product with a short life.

Materials   To the majority of people the word "fence" automatically means "made of wood." Most fences are. But we have had iron or steel fences for generations. And today, some fences are made of still other materials.

This wide choice adds substantially to the fun of fence building. If you have an idea for an unusual fence, the odds are heavily in your favor that you will be able to find just the right thing to build it with. But before you rush out and place an order, make sure that it has the characteristics required. These, of course, vary from project to project and also from one part of a fence to another. But as a general rule, all materials used must be

· Strong

· Resistant to the elements

· Resistant to decay

WOOD   The fact that wood continues to be the outstanding material for fence construction is evidence that it more than meets most requirements. Its only weakness—which you must never overlook—is its susceptibility to decay.

Ideally, all the wood in a fence should be decay-resistant; but since this runs up the cost, you can't be blamed for resisting the idea. It's silly, however, to take chances on the posts, because the portions buried in the ground will last only a few years if you use ordinary wood.

Redwood, cypress, and black locust have superior natural resistance to decay and are therefore usually the first choices for fence posts (but locust is used only for barbed wire and other farm fences). But you can do just as well with other woods such as pine

Five fence masterpieces from a bygone day. When these and others like them are gone, will they be no more? No, at a time when interest in the arts and crafts is soaring, there must be someone who will create new fence masterpieces. Maybe it will be you.

A fence from the era when gingerbread was in vogue.

and fir if you treat them with a wood preservative. In all cases, whether you use redwood or cypress or another wood, ask for timbers that are cut from the heartwood of the log, because this is less likely to rot than sapwood.

Lumber for a fence should have a nominal thickness of at least 1 in.—actual thickness of at least ¾ in. (All boards and timbers are identified by their nominal dimensions—1×8; 2×4; 4×4— whereas their actual dimensions are somewhat smaller—$¾ \times 7⅝$; $1⅝ \times 3⅝$; $3⅝ \times 3⅝$).

All timbers should be of construction grade; all boards of No. 3 Common grade if you don't mind large knots and some waste or of No. 2 Common grade otherwise.

PLYWOOD Plywood is used in a fence if you want large, unbroken panels or some of the special effects which are available only in plywood (for example, plywood surfaced with small stone chips to resemble coarse-aggregate concrete). Like solid wood, it can be painted, stained, or allowed to weather naturally.

Plywood of ¾-in. thickness can be used just like boards of the same thickness. In other words, if you build an 8-ft.-high fence, you

26

(Top) *This fence looks as if it were metal but it is really made of wood. The bowed pieces between the square pickets are lattice strips. The collars are made by cutting short lengths of wood molding; mitering the corners, and nailing them together.* (Bottom) *This fence is very similar to the one above. But instead of bowing lattice strips between the pickets, the designer formed diamonds.*

(Top) *This picket fence serves as the railing for the porch and obliterates the view (from the other side) of the ugly porch underpinnings. There is no set spacing for pickets in a fence. In some cases, the spaces are as wide as the pickets; but a closer spacing produces a prettier effect. Here the spaces are ¾ in. wide; the pickets, a nominal 3 in. wide.* (Bottom) *A combination barrier which is hard to beat for simple beauty: glistening white picket fence, gray stone wall, deep-green hemlock hedge. But there is one potential problem in planting an evergreen hedge close behind a fence like this: The fence cuts off the light from the hedge. So if the fence should ever be removed, a high strip of dead branches would be revealed.*

can install either boards or plywood on the same framework. It is also possible to use plywood in much thinner panels if you brace them adequately. For example, you can use ⅜-in. plywood provided you nail it to 2 × 4s spaced no more than 16 in. from center to center. Or you can use ½- or ⅝-in. plywood on 2 × 4s spaced up to 24 in. on centers.

But the single most important point to bear in mind when using plywood in a fence is that it must be of exterior grade. If an interior grade is used, the glue will fail and the plies separate.

HARDBOARD   Hardboard is a very hard, heavy, dense sheet material made of wood fibers bonded together under pressure. It is durable and strong; won't split, splinter, or crack; and has good resistance to moisture. Unlike its principal competitor, plywood, it doesn't stain well; but it's easy to paint, especially if the sheets have been finished at the factory with a baked-on prime coat (primed plywood is also sold).

Use only exterior grades in fences. Sheets up to ¼ in. thick must be braced with 2 × 4s spaced 16 in. on centers. For $\frac{5}{16}$-in. sheets, the spacing between timbers can be increased to 24 in.

ASBESTOS-CEMENT BOARD   This old but relatively unknown sheet material can be substituted for plywood or hardboard if you like its natural stone-gray color or want to paint the fence (it does not take stain). Made of asbestos fibers and Portland cement, the board is extremely heavy, dense and hard; and it is not only immune to fire and decay but also to just about every other problem.

Only $\frac{3}{16}$- or ¼-in.-thick boards should be used in a fence. The former should be nailed to 2× 4s spaced 16 in. on centers. The latter is suitable for 24-in. spacing.

FIBERGLASS   Fiberglass panels—as they are popularly known —are more properly called fiberglass-reinforced polyester panels because the principal ingredient is polyester. Most commonly used to roof terraces, they are very tough, strong, impact-, fire-, and weather-resistant sheets about 2 to 4 ft. wide and 8 to 12 ft. long. They come in a wide range of translucent colors.

Despite the fact that the material is only $\frac{1}{16}$ in. thick, corrugated panels up to 4 ft. wide can be used in fences without any bracing except around the perimeter. This is also true of flat panels, although in their case the maximum panel width is only 34 in.

GLASS   Glass is used in fences primarily when the homeowner wants a barrier which will admit a view; but occasionally textured

Two sides of a picket fence built to keep rabbits out of an outstanding garden. Surprisingly, chicken wire is applied to the front of the fence because it is usually seen only from a distance whereas the back of the fence, facing the garden, is seen close up. Below the bottom rail, wide boards set in trenches stymie the rabbits' attempts to dig under the fence. On the garden side, flowers and shrubs are so massed against the fence that in some places it is completely hidden.

A beautiful scallop-topped fence with square pickets.

or corrugated glass is used strictly for the decorative effect. In either case, glass is an expensive material; and because of its weight and breakability, large pieces should be installed by a professional —which adds further to its cost. Once in place, however, it will outlast the surrounding frame many times over. The only thing that can wreck it, short of a smashing blow, is wind-driven sand at a seashore.

In this fence the scallops are longer than the fence sections so the peaks do not fall directly above the posts.

Somewhat surprisingly, plate glass only ¼ in. thick can be used in larger pieces than the sheet materials mentioned above. The actual size of the pieces depends, however, on the strength of the wind buffeting them. For example, if the wind exerts an average pressure of 25 pounds per square foot, a single piece of ¼-in. plate which is reinforced only around the edges should not exceed 42 sq. ft. in area. By contrast, if the wind pressure is only 10 p.s.f., the glass area can be increased to about 100 sq. ft.

It's obvious from this that you should not build a glass fence without first determining the design load required by your local building code and then consulting a glass dealer to find which thickness and type of glass you should use. If the area of the panels you intend to install is fairly small, double-strength sheet glass can be used instead of plate—at a considerable saving in money. On the other hand, if your fence is exposed to very strong winds or is to be built with extremely large panels, you should use tempered

32

(Top) A high picket fence is bowed downward between the widely spaced brick piers. PHOTO BY WARWICK ANDERSON *(Bottom) Picket fences are not always low and white. This one is 5 ft. high and painted a black-green so it doesn't show dirt so badly.*

plate glass, which is about four times as strong as ordinary plate. (Even in modest sizes tempered glass should also be used in heavily traveled locations because, if someone crashes into it, it will disintegrate safely into tiny bits like rock salt.)

ACRYLIC   Acrylic is most widely used in transparent, colorless, glass-like sheets but is also available in many colors and textures. Of the various clear plastics, it is the best for outdoor use because it is strong, durable, weather-resistant, and little discolored by sunlight. Its only serious flaw is its rather poor resistance to abrasion. It is available in sheets up to 10×12 ft. and ranging from $\frac{3}{16}$ to $\frac{5}{8}$ in. thick. The largest sheet ($\frac{1}{2} \times 120 \times 144$ in.) will withstand winds of up to 20 p.s.f. if the four edges are set in channels (or between wood or metal stops) $1\frac{1}{4}$ in. deep. If $\frac{3}{16}$-in. material is used in a similar exposure, the maximum sheet size is 60×65 in.

PERFORATED METAL   This is an attractive material which is almost always overlooked as a fencing material despite the fact that it is often used in room dividers. Available in sheets up to 4×10 ft.,

34

it's no thicker than a coin yet has great strength and durability and requires only a light supporting frame. And it is made in a seemingly endless number of patterns.

Anodized aluminum should be used if you want a natural finish. Steel can be used for painting, although aluminum is preferable since you don't have to touch it up the instant the paint is knicked.

FASTENERS The fasteners for a fence include all the nails, screws, bolts, angle irons, etc., used to put it together. By and large, galvanized steel is the best choice because it is resistant to rusting and is inexpensive. Brass and aluminum are even better, but cost more and are not made in every type of fastener you are likely to need.

Never use ordinary steel, because it rusts almost instantly, leaves brown stains on the surrounding surfaces, and eventually disintegrates.

Using Wood Preservatives

Wood preservatives make it possible to slow the decay of ordinary wood and plywood so they will last as long as redwood and cypress; and they add much less to the cost of a fence than the two latter materials. But to be effective, you must choose and apply them carefully.

Old-fashioned creosote is still as good as anything for the buried portions of fence posts. But it may kill any vegetation in the immediate vicinity; and if used above ground, it discolors the wood and bleeds through paint which is applied over it.

Pentachlorophenol and copper-naphthanate are more widely used because they do not cause such problems. However, if you intend to paint wood which has been treated with them, you must select a formulation which can be painted over. Not all qualify; in fact, the best preservatives for the buried ends of posts are made with a fairly heavy oil vehicle which prevents paint from sticking tight.

Application of wood preservative should be made only to clean lumber *after* all cutting, drilling, and shaping have been completed. If you use a paint brush, slather the preservative on every inch of the wood; let it soak in; and slather on some more. The more you apply, the better the protection.

A superior method of treating the ends of fence posts is to soak them in preservative for 24 hours or more. But to do this, you need a vessel which has a depth equal to the depth of the postholes; and

35

One of the prettiest types of fence is made with slender square or round pickets which are usually separated by spaces equal to about twice their width. In this very simple design, the pickets are nailed to the front of the rails.

the most obvious thing—a 50-gal. drum—would cost a fortune to fill. Perhaps you can find something smaller.

Making Concrete Fence Posts

You don't see concrete fence posts very much these days. In the past, they were more popular. I could make a guess at what brought the change, but it would be only a guess.

In any event, concrete posts should not be ignored just because they have been given the cold shoulder by modern fence builders. Their durability is unmatched. You don't have to paint or finish them. And their appearance may be just right for your plans.

You can easily make your own posts. For round posts, buy fiber forms which are designed specifically for the purpose. Cut them to the proper length; stand them upright and brace them; insert three ¼-in. steel reinforcing rods ¾ in. from the sides; and pour in the concrete.

To make square posts—say, four at a time—build wood forms on a piece of ¾-in. plywood. Cut five smooth-sided 2 × 4s to the length of the post and lay them on the plywood, thin edge up, in parallel rows 3⅝ in. apart—thus forming a series of four troughs. Nail boards across the ends of the 2 × 4s to hold them together. Finally, to prevent the outer timbers from spreading, nail blocks of wood against them and to the plywood.

If you don't want square corners on the posts, nail ⅝-in. cove moldings into each section of the form. The moldings, cut to the length of the posts, are tacked into the bottom corners of each trough and to the sides at the top of the trough.

Brush clean motor oil, cut with an equal amount of kerosene, on all surfaces of the forms so the concrete won't stick to them.

Mix 1 part Portland cement with 2 parts sand and 2½ parts clean gravel not over ¾-in. diameter. Add water to make a workable but not soupy mix. Then pour an inch of concrete into the bottom of each form. On this lay two ¼-in. reinforcing rods ¾ in. from the sides. The rods should be about 1½ in. shorter than the posts and centered between the ends. Then fill each form to within ¾ in. of the top with additional concrete, and lay in two more reinforcing rods before filling in all the way with concrete. As the concrete is placed in a form, run a mason's trowel along the sides and up and down in the concrete to remove air bubbles (but take care not to disturb the reinforcement). Finally, strike the concrete off flush with the top edges of the form.

In this long fence with
square pickets of alternating
height, the pickets appear
to be set into the center of
the rails. Actually they are
nailed to the front of the
rails and moldings are
applied over them.

Unlike square pickets, round pickets are inserted in holes in the rails. Note how this fence is stepped down a slight slope. There is only one change in the height of the top and middle rails (the highest section at the fence is a driveway gate). But the height of the bottom rail changes from section to section.

Bolts, angle irons, etc., which will attach the fence rails or panels to the posts should now be inserted in the concrete. Make sure they are properly spaced and securely anchored. Firm the concrete around them and resmooth the surface.

Let the concrete set until firm, then cover it with wet burlap for a couple of days. After that, you can remove the forms but should continue to keep the posts covered with wet burlap (or simply spray them twice a day) for the next eight days.

Round posts are allowed to cure for at least four days before the fiber tubes are cut from top to bottom and peeled off. Keep the posts damp for a week thereafter.

Don't set any concrete post in the ground until it has cured for a total of four weeks.

Laying Out a Fence

You should never try to lay out a fence by eye. Use a 50- or 100-ft. steel tape to make measurements; strong white twine to mark the position of the fence; smooth, narrow, pointed boards or pieces of broom handles or brass curtain rods for stakes. (Stakes cut from tree limbs or rough-split from boards are hard to drive straight and can throw off your measurements.)

When laying out a division fence, don't assume that you know where the boundary line lies. Take a look at your plot plan: You may find the line is not at all where you thought it to be. You may find it isn't even straight.

When you go outdoors, make sure that the pipes or other markers indicating your line are the right ones. Many strange things happen to boundary line markers. They get pulled out, driven below ground, moved. New pipes which can be mistaken for the old are often added in out-of-the-way places. The only way you can be certain about the position of a boundary is to study your property map and use a tape to verify the markers you find. If you can't find any markers, hire a surveyor.

Putting heads together with your neighbor may seem to be a sensible way to locate a common boundary; but he may not know any more about it than you do. So if the two of you decide the line is a foot closer to your house than it actually is, you lose the use (though not the ownership) of a bit of property when you build the fence. Or if you build the fence closer to your neighbor's house than you should, you may spend money planting property that isn't yours; and when your neighbor moves, the surveyor for the new buyer is bound to find the fence is in the wrong spot and his client may appropriate it, destroy it, or insist you move it.

In short, it takes care to lay out a division fence.

Other types of fences generally do not require the same care. Even so, if a fence is supposed to deviate from a straight line, you want to be sure—for appearance's sake, if for nothing else—that it conforms to the plan you have drawn for it.

This is a round-picket fence similar to the preceding. But each section is exactly like the next, and each steps down an inch or two from the one before. Another slight difference between this and the preceding fence is in the position of the intermediate rail and the height of the intermediate pickets.

Suppose the fence turns a 90° corner. To assure that the corner actually is a right angle, nail three boards together into a triangle with sides of 3, 4, and 5 ft. After establishing the location of one run of fence and marking it with a string, place the triangle at the corner point with the 3-ft. side parallel to the string. Then draw a second string taut over the 4-ft. side. The angle formed by the strings is exactly 90°.

To form an angle other than a right angle, draw it first on paper. Then build a large wooden triangle to corresponding dimensions. Lay this on the ground and stretch strings over the short legs.

If a fence is to be laid out in an arc, establish the ends of the

The posts in this square-picket fence are much more substantial—in keeping with the design of the house—than those in similar fences shown. The spaces below the bottom rails are enclosed by boards resting on long square-cut stones. Placing a continuous row of cut stones or bricks under a fence was a common practice in old city fences.

A lovely fence atop a stone retaining wall protects anyone who walks on the hillside against a dangerous tumble.

arc and drive stakes into the ground at these points. Then stretch a string between the stakes and find the middle.

To draw the arc, tie one end of a second long string to a spike, round curtain rod, or slender plumbing pipe. Drive the spike into the ground at the middle of the first string; pull the string that is tied to it out to one of the stakes; wrap the string around a pointed stick or wood; and sweep it around to the other stake, scratching a line in the ground. The result is a perfect semicircle.

If the arc is deeper than you want, lay a wooden right triangle (like that used for making a 90° corner) at right angles to the mid-point of the first string; and draw a long line perpendicular to the string. Then drive the spike attached to the second string into the ground somewhere along this perpendicular line, pull the string out to one of the stakes, and sweep it around to the other stake. This establishes a somewhat shallower arc.

If you're still not satisfied with the arc, move the spike further out along the perpendicular line to produce a shallower arc; or move it further in toward the middle of the first string to produce a deeper arc.

Locating Fence Posts

Two preliminary comments are in order:

1. In most fences, the sections are 8 ft. long (measured from the *center* to one post to the *center* of the next). But you can make the sections any length you like. For instance, you might use 10-ft. sections in a rail fence. On the other hand, if a fence is solid and exposed to high winds, you should probably shorten the sections to 6 ft. in order to give greater stability. Short sections may also be advisable if the ground is very sandy or turns into soupy clay in wet weather; or if the fence borders a busy sidewalk.

Another reason for using some spacing other than 8 ft. between posts is because the total length of a fence is not exactly divisible by eight. For example, if your lot is 107 ft. wide and you want the fence to stretch from sideline to sideline, a fence with 8-ft. sections must include one 3-ft. section. In a solid-board fence, this short section would not be noticeable except to someone behind the fence. But in most other types of fence, the short section would stand out; so to prevent this, you should change the length of all the sections to 8 ft. 3 in. or perhaps 9 ft. 10½ in.

2. On flat land or very gently sloping or undulating land, fences usually follow the contours of the land; that is, the top of the fence

runs parallel with the ground. On hillsides, however, the top of the fence is usually horizontal; and the fence is built like a flight of steps simply because it looks better—especially in a built-up neighborhood where the viewer is surrounded by houses with definite horizontal and vertical lines.

Admittedly, not all fence builders follow these practices. In this book there are pictures of "stepped" fences on slight slopes and of "follow-the-land" fences on rather steep slopes. Since none of these is unattractive, you can't say the builders were wrong. And you won't necessarily be wrong if you also deviate from the "rules." But if in doubt, don't.

All of which brings us finally to the first step in the actual construction of a fence—locating the posts.

If a fence is to follow the contours of the land, drive stakes into the ground to mark the centers of the two end posts, and stretch a string between them. Then, starting at either end, measure to

Here the square pickets terminate below the top rail but extend through the bottom rail.

(Top) *The balustrade on the steps and entrance platform continues around the front of the house as a fence. The top rail is rounded for appearances and to shed water.* (Bottom) *Another balustrade-like fence with wood cutouts inserted between the pickets under the top rail.*

This long horizontal board fence helps to make the rather tall house, set close behind, look lower.

the center of the next post and drive a stake, and continue thus until all post positions are established.

The technique for staking out a stepped fence is quite different. First, locate the end post at the top of the hill, and drive in a stake. Fasten a string to the top of the stake and pull it out level for the length of the fence section. Use a carpenter's level to make certain the string is horizontal. Then drop a plumb line to the ground and drive in a stake to mark the center of the second post.

Now tie the string to stake no. 2; pull it out level; drop your plumb line; and drive in a stake for the third post.

And so on to the downhill end of the fence.

Locating posts for a curving fence (which is usually built on flat land) starts with drawing the arc of the fence on the ground. Drive in a stake for one of the end posts. Then curve a tape measure along the arc for the required distance, set the next stake, and proceed on around to the last stake.

Another horizontal board fence made in longer sections and with wider boards. A luxuriant bed of red, pink, and white begonias is planted at the base.

Digging Postholes and Setting Posts

The main reason why so many fences seem to be on the verge of collapse is that they were built by lazybones. I may sound like a slave driver, but the plain truth is that if you want a fence to stand up to the constant beating it receives from wind, people, animals, and machines, the posts must be set in the ground to a depth of 24 to 36 in. Thirty inches is an excellent average—the depth I always recommend.

The mere thought of such a hole may make you weary, but if you don't try to dig all the holes for a fence at once, you should survive the exercise with vigor to spare.

Use a posthole digger—not an ordinary garden spade. For one thing, it is easier to handle because it is specially designed for the job. For another thing, it makes a much narrower hole than a shovel, and this helps to hold the posts upright.

Of the two muscle-driven posthole diggers that are used, the more common is the clamshell type with two handles and two

51

A high three-rail board fence follows the contours of the land on a Tennessee horse farm. The round posts are partially concealed by vertical boards nailed over joints in the fence. The boards also help to anchor the rails in case they're kicked by a horse.

Board fence in a diamond pattern. The tops of the posts are cut at an acute angle to shed water.

(Top) *In this board fence the tops of the posts are not only angled but also covered with strips of aluminum flashing which extend over the joints in the rails to keep out water.*

PHOTO BY WARWICK ANDERSON (Center) *Crossbuck fences have a neat, geometric precision.* (Bottom) *This advanced version of a crossbuck fence is hardly easy to build, but mighty attractive.*

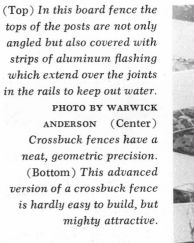

The hurdle fence is a rustic type made with small rails strengthened by diagonal bracing.

narrow, spade-like blades which are hinged together. It is ideal for digging holes in rough, stony New England soil, and is equally good in other soils in all other parts of the country. However, in firm soil which is free of stones, the auger type of digger is not only easier to work but also makes a smaller (6-in.) hole.

Power-driven augers are used when there are lots of holes to dig. The one and only time I ever used one was to dig holes in dense clay. It was a disastrous experience. I think I'm strong but I just couldn't control the machine. I drilled one-and-a-half holes; shut it off; scraped off the clay; and returned it to the rental agency. The rest of the holes I dug with a clamshell digger.

But I don't want to downgrade power augers too badly. They wouldn't exist if they didn't work. Perhaps the secret is to begin with a two-man machine and shift to a one-man model later.

Regardless of the posthole digger you use, you may need several other tools to get the job done: a crowbar to dislodge boulders; a jackhammer to break through ledge rock; a spade to refill the holes when the posts are set.

Once the holes are dug a little deeper than the required 30-in. depth, pour 2 to 4 in. of small rocks in the bottoms so water will not stand around the ends of the posts. Tamp firm. Set in the posts

56

(Top) *A high, closely spaced picket fence in Ste. Genevieve, Missouri. (Bottom) On a hillside lot a fence need not be the same height at all places to give privacy in the yard. This new board fence is much higher at the uphill end of the lot than at the downhill end, where a low fence topping a retaining wall gives equal protection. The tops of the palings are rounded like the lights in the fan window in the gable.*

(Top) A slat fence, so-called because it is made of narrow boards with slight spaces between. The slats are centered on the top and bottom rails. (Bottom) Each section of the diagonal boards in this redwood fence between a patio and utility area are set in "picture-frame" panels made of 2 x 4s. The posts and rails are 4 x 6s and are held together by large angle irons.

PHOTO BY THE CALIFORNIA REDWOOD ASSOCIATION

(Top) *"Window fence" permits the homeowners to lounge on the terrace while keeping an eye on youngsters in the swimming pool. The windows are also used for displaying potted and hanging plants.* PHOTO BY THE CALIFORNIA REDWOOD ASSOCIATION (Bottom) *Contrary to general practice, the back of this board fence was faced to the street. Then the owners made amends to the public by painting the posts and rails white and staining the boards dark brown. The result is very pleasing.*

Four-foot fence of solid boards keeps children from straying into the pool area, as the law requires, and is infinitely more attractive than the chain-link fences usually used for the purpose. PHOTO BY MILLARD J. MEYERS FOR PRINCE HILL POOLS

Board fence with a short picketed top nailed to the back. The owners evidently did not want to replace the old stone end post but did want a fence higher than the post; hence the reduction in elevation. Unfortunately, the boards at this end of the fence rotted out near the bottom; and instead of replacing them, the owners nailed plywood over them. But the repair is hardly more noticeable to passersby than to the camera.

and measure the projections above ground. The posts may need to be raised slightly or shortened. If cutting is necessary, do it now while the posts are loose and can be laid across a pair of sawhorses. Trying to cut off the tops of posts stuck firmly in the ground is difficult.

If your soil is reasonably compact, just packing it into the holes

A multilevel deck surrounded with three types of tall redwood fence. That in the foreground is made with wide boards set edge to edge; that in the background, with narrow boards spaced about 1½ in. apart. The fence behind the birch is a latticework made of 2- x 3-in. verticals nailed between the top and bottom rails and 1- x 2-in. horizontals nailed flush with the faces of the rails and posts. The openings in the lattice are about 4 in. square. PHOTO BY ERNEST BRAUN FOR THE CALIFORNIA REDWOOD ASSOCIATION

White board fence atop a stone-masonry wall. The ends are rounded.

around the posts will provide all the support that's necessary. Fill in about 6 in. at a time; ram it down with a 2 × 4; and add another 6 in. If you have stones, wedge some of them in around the posts for good measure. When you finally reach grade level, slope the soil away from the posts so water won't stand around them.

Setting posts in concrete is necessary only if the soil is very sandy or very clayey and/or if the fence is exposed to hard winds or possible traffic damage. In any of these cases, filling a standard-diameter posthole with concrete generally provides all the stability required. But if a fence is very high, heavy, and solid, it's advisable to enlarge the upper half of the holes to about twice standard diameter.

First pour a layer of small stones in the bottom of a hole. After dropping in the post, fill around it with another 2 or 3 in. of stones. Then shovel in concrete made of 1 part Portland cement, 3 parts sand, 4 parts small gravel, and enough water to make a rather dry

A fence to marvel at. In almost 40 years I have never seen it in anything except apple-pie condition.

mix. Work a broom handle up and down in the poured concrete to eliminate air pockets. If you want to make the concrete go a little further, drop in a few large, well-washed rocks. At the top of the hole, form the concrete into a shallow cone sloping away from the post in all directions. If the fence is to be surrounded with grass, the concrete should be exposed so you won't have to mow or clip up close to the post. In a cultivated planting bed, however, the concrete should be cut off just below the soil surface: It isn't very pretty.

64

The upper step-down-the-hill fence shields a small terrace from the immediately adjacent street. Tall fences which were solid at the bottom and open at the top were rather common in the past and are still sometimes built. The owner of the lower fence is doing everything possible to keep it from being knocked down by errant motorists and cyclists: Note the ornamental steel straps which help to anchor the posts to the brick base (into which the straps are inserted vertically).

Board-and-board fence looks the same on both sides. It is made of 8-in. boards spaced 6 in. apart. The boards on one side are centered on the spaces on the other side. Result: a good wind and privacy screen.

This board-and-board fence in the center of a town is made of rough-sawn cedar boards which are weathering naturally. Since privacy is more important here than in the preceding suburban garden, the boards are more closely spaced. As shown in the closeup, you can see through the fence only if you stand at the right angle; but you can't see much even so.

(Top) A prefabricated basket-weave fence sold through mail-order and building supplies outlets. Though much less attractive than the basket-weave fence on page 21, it is easier to erect. (Bottom) Louvered fences are fair windbreaks, and block the view from all angles except one. The louvers are 6-in. boards set at a 45° angle between 2 x 4 rails. For ease of installation, nail 1- x 4-in. boards to the rails between each pair of louvers, and drive nails diagonally through these spacers and the louvers into the rails.

Lining Up Posts

The hardest part of fence building is to align the posts so that each is straight up and down and all are in a straight row.

The best way to go about this is to set the end posts first. As you fill in around them, check them frequently with a carpenter's level to make sure they are as straight as a rocket on its launch pad. Then stretch two strings between them—one at the top, the other about 1 ft. off the ground. Tack them to the sides of the posts.

Set the intermediate posts so they just touch the strings; and use a carpenter's level to see that they don't slant to either side.

The 2 x 6 louvers in this fence around a sunbathing terrace are pivoted so they can be opened (individually) by hand to any desired degree for air circulation, closed tight for privacy. The pivots are lag bolts driven through the top and bottom rails. So they can clear one another, the louvers are slightly shaped along the edges.

Wood Fence Construction

Although fences are built in many slightly different ways, depending on the design, three basic construction methods are used:

SOLID, SLAT, AND PICKET FENCES These are built with 4- × 4-in. posts and 2- × 4-in. rails. After a pair of posts is in place, the bottom rail is set between them, leveled, and fastened by driving 3-in. galvanized nails diagonally through the ends into the posts. If necessary, angle irons can be added for reinforcement.

The top rail is either installed in the same way or nailed across the tops of the posts. The latter installation is simpler to make and also helps to stiffen a fence since each section of top rail is usually long enough to stretch over three posts.

Palings are nailed to the sides of the rails and posts. They should be spaced so all posts are concealed behind them.

If solid panels or boards are installed within the frame formed

A favorite in times past, this is still a charming type of fence. It consists of turned wood posts with "diamond-shaped" rails mortised into the sides.

(Top) *Four-foot fence faced with clapboards is almost indistinguishable from the house. It surrounds a narrow terrace in front of the windows and door.* (Bottom) *Screen fence made of 1- x 1-in. redwood strips spaced ½ in. apart and nailed to 2 x 4 rails which are partially mortised into the posts.* PHOTO BY THE CALIFORNIA REDWOOD ASSOCIATION

Beautiful patterning in the old fence in front of the Henry Wadsworth Long-fellow home in Cambridge, Massachusetts. It was vandalized the night before this picture was taken. PHOTO BY THOMAS P. ROONEY

In contrast with the Long-fellow fence's Chinese Chippendale motif, this one in Connecticut looks as if it might have been built by a Navajo blanket weaver.

(Top) *This high, short fence section was designed mostly for effect but does help to screen the entrance court from the driveway. It is made of 1- x 4-in. boards which are separated and braced by wood blocks of random sizes set in a random pattern.* (Bottom) *An interesting way to provide privacy for a swimming pool built close to a street: Louvered shutters set into the brick wall allow air circulation while preventing passersby from peering in.* PHOTO BY THE NATIONAL SWIMMING POOL INSTITUTE

by the posts and rails, grooves to receive them are cut in the top of the bottom rail and bottom of the top rail with an electric router (in which case, the top rail is not nailed to the posts until the panel is in place). The alternative—which uses more lumber but does not require a router—is to sandwich the top and bottom edges of the panels between moldings nailed to the inside horizontal faces of the rails.

HORIZONTAL BOARD FENCES These are among the easiest fences to build because after the 4- $\times$ 4-in. posts are set, you simply nail the rails, which are 1-in.-thick boards, to the front side. To give the fence greater stiffness, stagger the joints in the top and bottom rails. In other words, if the fence is made in 8-ft. sections, start the top rail with a 16-ft. board; the bottom rail with an 8-ft. board. Continue from there with 16-ft. boards for both rails until you reach the other end of the fence, where you finish the top rail with an 8-ft. board.

If the fence has additional rails, stagger the joints in these also.

POST-AND-RAIL FENCE This type of fence is almost always built with precut rails that slide loosely into holes in precut posts. In the popular rustic version of the fence, the rails are split from logs and the large posts are either split or hand-hewn logs. In more refined fences, the rails and posts are either round or square.

To build a post-and-rail fence, set one end post solidly into the ground; but instead of filling in around the other end post, brace it upright with three diagonal boards nailed to the sides and driven into the ground. Tie two strings to the sides of the posts to help in leveling the intermediate posts; but for the moment, leave the intermediate posts loose in their holes.

Slip the rails into the solid end post and into the second (adjacent) post. Plumb the second post and hold it upright with a diagonal brace driven into the ground at right angles to the fence. Then install the next set of rails between the second and third posts, and brace the third post. Now return to the second post, align it with the strings and make sure it doesn't slant sideways; and fill in around the base. Then fit the rails between the third and fourth posts. Brace the fourth post and fill in around the third post.

Repeat this process to the end of the fence. To fit the rails into the final end post, you must remove the braces on it.

There are two reasons for following this procedure, which is less complicated than it sounds. First, it is obviously impossible to insert

A zigzag, or Virginia rail, fence requires no foundations, no posts, no nails— just sections of split logs.
PHOTO BY WARWICK
ANDERSON

(Top) A two-rail post-and-rail fence with split rails and hand-hewn posts. PHOTO BY WARWICK ANDERSON (Center) A refined post-and-rail fence with square posts and rails (which are installed diagonally). (Bottom) In this white-painted post-and-rail fence, the posts are round and the rails are made of small whole logs.

To reduce costs to customers, few building supplies outlets offer three-hole posts for post-and-rail fences any longer; but such posts are still available if you shop for them. This fence is built with split rails and split posts.

(Right) *Decorative highway safety fence is equally suitable for hazardous driveways and turnarounds. This also is a post-and-rail fence.* (Opposite, top) *How to keep livestock from escaping over a low stone wall—an old solution: Nail or wire pairs of posts into a triangle placed over the wall and set red cedar saplings across the top.* (Opposite, bottom) *Splendid homemade post-and-rail fence takes its design from that of the owner's house (not shown), which is a replica of our earliest New England homes. Heavy wire mesh is nailed to the fence to keep varmints out of the vegetable garden.*

rails into two adjacent posts which are set firmly in the ground. One of them must be loose. Second, if the rails do not fit properly in the intermediate posts, the posts may slant sideways. But by leaving the posts loose, you can adjust the rails or even cut a little off the ends so the posts will be vertical.

Fence made of woven saplings lighted by night. The sections are fastened to wood rails on the back side. PHOTO BY JOHN WATSON, LANDSCAPE ILLUMINATOR

Weatherproofing Wood Fences

Despite the fact that a fence is a slender vertical structure with few horizontal surfaces, decay often sets in above ground in places where for one reason or another rain becomes trapped. This is not altogether preventable but the problem can—and should—be minimized during the construction process by taking two steps:

1. Brush wood preservative on all surfaces where one board or timber overlaps another, so that water dripping into the joint will not do any damage. For example, you should apply preservative to the ends of rails and the sides of posts where they join. Similarly, you should apply preservative to the sides of rails and the backs of palings where they join.

2. Bevel the tops of rails, posts, and palings slightly so water will run off.

82

(Top) *Modern stockade fences are reasonably inexpensive and useful as privacy fences, but there's nothing pretty about them and they are being used so indiscriminately that they have become deadly boring.* PHOTO BY THE JACOBSEN MANUFACTURING COMPANY (Bottom) *A more finished version of a stockade fence made with turned rather than rustic palings and with a cap rail at the top.*

A modern copy of the early stockade fences which were built to keep out marauders. Note how much more substantial it is than the prefab fences now sold.

Old-time fence-builders often went one step beyond this by nailing slanting or rounded drip caps to the tops of fences from one end to the other.

Finishing Wood Fences

Some fences are simply left to weather naturally. The result is an attractive but uneven silvery-gray color. But the color comes slowly. To speed the process, you can apply a bleaching oil containing gray pigment to a new fence. The pigment produces an instantaneous weathered look. By the time this wears away, the bleaching agent, working with the sun and rain, have taken effect.

If you want to change the color of a fence without concealing

This stockade fence was so depressing to my wife and me when we bought our home that we intended to rip it out. But other jobs had priority, so in the interim we decided to take the curse off it by painting it white and planting Hicks yews in front. It is still no thing of beauty but is so improved that it's still with us.

A strictly utilitarian fence of log slabs.

Rough, unfinished wood
strips are strung together—
but not quite touching—on
iron pipes installed between
square stone posts. If you
need a curving fence, this
is one way to build it.

the grain or texture of the wood, apply two coats of a transparent oil stain. The second coat should be applied within thirty minutes of the first for best results. On rough-sawn wood, the color will last eight to ten years before refinishing (with one coat) is called for. On smooth wood, the stain has a life of only about four years.

A painted fence requires more maintenance but produces the greatest change in appearance. Apply an oil-base exterior primer first and complete the job with a coat of oil-base exterior trim paint. Because this has a gloss finish, dirt does not cling to it as tenaciously as to a flat finish. Even so, a fence under trees needs annual washing to keep it clean and reasonably new looking. Repainting is necessary after about four or five years.

Building a Curved Fence

The difficult part of building this kind of fence is to construct the rails. The ideal procedure is to have them fabricated at a mill or to cut them yourself out of 2- $\times$ 12-in. timbers with a saber saw or band saw. Once they are toenailed between the posts, you can apply palings either over them (as in a picket fence) or between them (as in a louvered fence). The only drawback is the cost.

A less expensive procedure is to make the rails out of three thicknesses of 1- $\times$ 3-in. D Select softwood boards which are coated with wood preservative and nailed together face to face.

For posts, use 4- $\times$ 6-in. timbers and cut rectangular notches in the narrow front faces to receive the rails. After setting the posts and filling in around them, brace them from behind with a couple of diagonal boards driven into the ground. Then nail a 1 $\times$ 3 from post to post to form the back of the top rail, and nail two additional

Curved fence around a terrace is assembled from narrow aluminum panels of several widths, four textures, and with gold or yellow anodized finishes. Mesh panels are interspersed with the solid panels to admit air and a limited view.
PHOTO BY JULIUS SHULMAN FOR THE ALUMINUM COMPANY OF AMERICA

1×3s on top of this to complete the rail. Assemble the bottom rail in the same way.

There are two ways to achieve the proper curve in the built-up, or laminated, rails. One is to lay the first 1×3 on the ground; bend it to the curve scratched in the ground; and nail a brace across the top edge to maintain the curve until the board is nailed to the posts. The other method is to mark the length of the fence sections on a 1×3; then nail one end of the board to the first post; bend it until the mark is centered in the notch in the second post; and then nail it to the second post. In either case, once the first board in each rail is bent and nailed in place, the other boards are readily bent and nailed over it.

After the framework of a curved fence is completed, nail the palings or panels to the front edges of the rails. If you use palings, select the narrowest strips which are suitable to your design because they will form a more nearly perfect curve than wide boards. For panels, use either hardboard or asbestos-cement board, both of which are readily bowed without special treatment. Plastic panels are equally bendable.

Don't remove the braces from the fence posts for about two months after completion of the fence. They are needed to resist the efforts of the rails to straighten themselves.

Building an Iron Fence

Unless you take up blacksmithing, the only thing you have to do to build an iron fence is to install the sections delivered from the fabricator.

To hold the fence upright, the posts should be embedded in concrete piers sunk at least 18 in. below grade in frost-free climates; below the frost line elsewhere. The easiest way to construct these is to dig holes with a clamshell-type posthole digger and fill them with concrete made to the 1-3-4 formula given earlier. Set in the posts to the desired depth while the concrete is soft. To keep the fence from sinking deeper under its own weight, place blocks of wood or bricks under the bottom rail; and hold the fence upright —after plumbing it carefully—with diagonal boards extending to either side of the fence. Lash the braces to the fence and drive the other ends into the ground. Then pack the concrete firmly around the posts and slant the top away from them slightly.

If a fence is to be erected atop a brick or stone wall, drill holes 3 in. deep with a carbide-tipped electric drill or star drill. Make the

An assortment of old iron fences. They were perhaps overly ornate. And they are unquestionably a frightful chore to scrape and paint. But they are knockouts— worth whatever it costs to salvage or duplicate them.

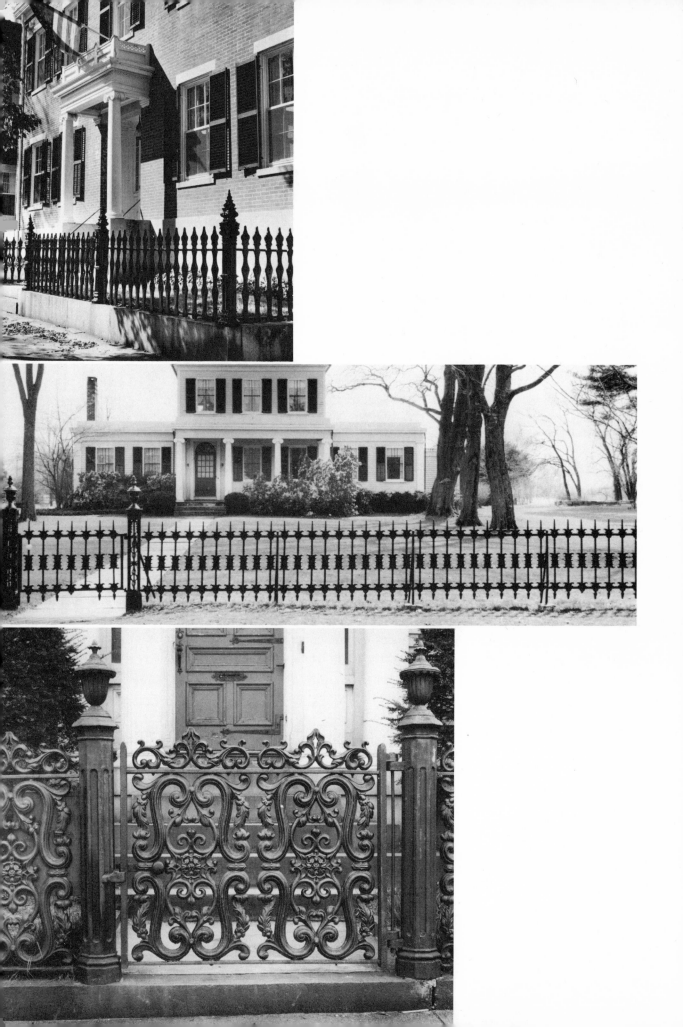

Iron fence and gate of extremely delicate design.

holes at least ½ in. wider than the posts. Then set the posts and pack a quick-setting cement in around them.

Another way to anchor posts is to set them in steel flanges made for the purpose. These are screwed to lead expansion anchors which are set into holes drilled in the top of the wall. The posts are then simply slipped into the flanges.

Iron fences are attached at the ends to masonry or stone posts with heavy-duty angle irons supplied by the fence fabricator. The irons are screwed to lead anchors recessed in the posts; and the fence rails are then bolted to them.

An important step in erecting all iron fences is to coat them thoroughly with a red-lead primer before they are erected, because rust may set in overnight if they are exposed to the slightest dampness—and once that happens, you are in for an unpleasant lot of scraping and sanding. I don't even trust the primer which may be applied by the fabricator (unless it is red lead). For a final finish, apply one or two coats of oil-base exterior trim paint.

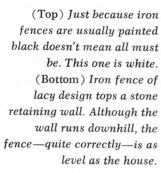

(Top) Just because iron fences are usually painted black doesn't mean all must be. This one is white. (Bottom) Iron fence of lacy design tops a stone retaining wall. Although the wall runs downhill, the fence—quite correctly—is as level as the house.

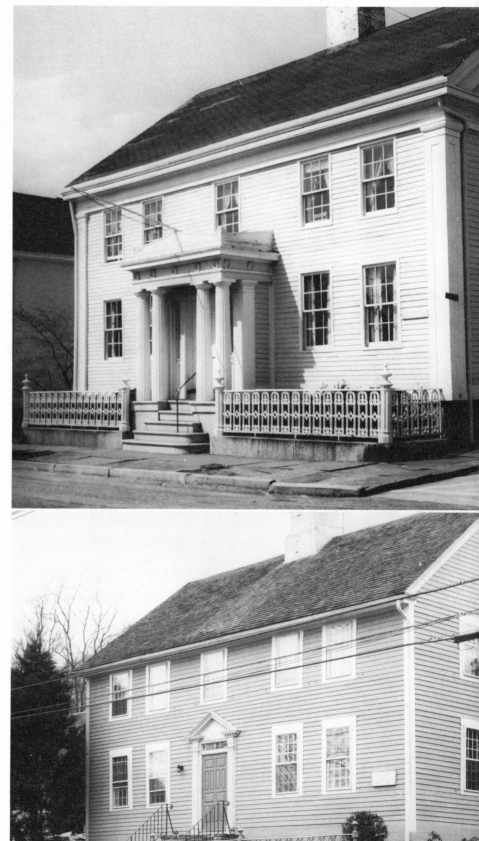

(Right) *Modern iron fence in a diamond pattern. The gate is similarly patterned but is made of much heavier metal.* (Opposite) *Iron fence surmounting a stone retaining wall separates a lawn area from a lower area planted to flowers and flowering shrubs.*

Building Steel-mesh Fences

Erecting a chain-link fence is one job the amateur should not undertake because it takes experience to stretch the mesh tight. Let the supplier do it for you.

Other mesh is lighter and therefore easier to work with. But to save time and work, some people make the mistake of supporting the wire entirely on the posts. This just doesn't work, because no matter how stiff the mesh may seem, it bellies badly between the posts without anything to stiffen it.

The proper framework for a mesh fence is like that for a wood fence—consisting of 4- × 4-in. posts and 2- × 4-in. top and bottom rails. The mesh is then fastened to the rails with large galvanized staples spaced about 1 ft. apart. To pull the mesh taut and smooth, rent or buy a stretching clamp which attaches to the mesh and a fence stretcher which is hooked to the clamp and, at the other end, to a tree or other stationary object.

If the purpose of a mesh fence is to keep a dog penned up or to keep animal pests out of a vegetable garden, the lower edge should

Translucent plastic panels set in a light timber frame obscure vision but allow you to see the shape of things set close to the other side. Even on the north side of the fence, plants get ample light to grow and bloom.

be sunk in the ground 4 to 6 in. As an additional safeguard, dig the trench about 3 in. deeper than the mesh, and fill it with concrete extending up around the mesh for a couple of inches.

Since mesh fences are galvanized, they don't need to be painted immediately; but in time they will show rusty patches. Rust or not, however, such fences are less objectionable when they are painted to blend into the landscape from the outset.

Use an oil-base exterior trim paint. Of the many application methods favored by professional and amateur painters, the easiest is to use a long-napped paint roller. Roll slowly to avoid splatter, and touch up the spots you miss with a brush.

4 Wall Building

The last wall I built was 6 ft. high, 40 ft. long, and made of stone and mortar. I started it in the early fall and didn't finish until the following summer. Time was lost because of freezing weather; still, it was a massive and at times grueling undertaking which I didn't make any easier by my insistence (inspired by a meager bank account) on using only stones I could collect from the surrounding countryside. Even in rock-strewn Connecticut, finding good stones large enough to make a visual and voluminous impression in the wall but small enough to load into my poor old car soon proved to be far more difficult than I had anticipated.

But when the wall was finally done, I had nothing but pride in my accomplishment. It was a good-looking—no, handsome—barrier, and as solid as Gibraltar. Today, 25 years later, it is as good as ever and has gained in beauty under its acquired encrustation of lichens. Perhaps more to the point, my enthusiasm for wall building has soared. True, I have not built any new walls, because I didn't and don't need them. But in winter, when the garden is under wraps, my favorite noon pastime is to rebuild the old dry walls which man, nature, and animals have partially demolished in the meadow behind my home.

Wall building is splendid exercise. More than that, it is a fascination. I cannot explain this. But to the horror of one of my editors, I liken it to eating peanuts. One o'clock comes. One-fifteen. I should be getting back to my typewriter. I'll lay up just one more stone, I tell myself. But the minutes tick by as one more stone follows another.

Dry Stone Walls

Lyme, Connecticut, where I live today, is one stone wall after another. In a rude, plebeian way, they must be counted among man's most beautiful artistic efforts. They have a stability and solidity which seem almost to have disappeared from this fragile world. In their gray, fissured, lichen-covered sides is the texture of a rich Oriental rug. No other structures blend so well with nature.

Most of our Lyme walls are ancient, but there are plenty of new ones, too. Just a few months ago, about a mile down the road, an unknown neighbor was building one. I doubt that he had ever done such a thing before. But if he didn't know exactly what he was about, he had the good sense to make haste slowly. Time after time when I passed him, I saw him carefully trying this stone and that. And when he finally finished the wall, he had built a small masterpiece—every bit as good as many of those put up by the experts of the 1700s.

One reason for the young man's success was that he had bought a small load of stones to supplement those he found on his own property and in the woods behind. Good wall-building stones, as I said earlier, don't grow everywhere in plentiful supply. Right here in Lyme, for instance, there are areas with nothing but the rounded boulders left by the glaciers—these are extremely difficult to build

Two-tier New England stone wall is 6 ft. wide in spots. The large rocks in the tiers are sloped slightly toward the center of the wall, and the space between is filled with small stones.

with—while there are other areas with striated ledges which yield the finest flat building blocks anyone could ask for.

Now, of course, you can build a wall with any kind of stone, but unless you're forced to pinch pennies hard, there's no point in struggling with shapeless chunks which not only don't want to stay in place but also give the finished wall an ugly, jumbled look. Use flatter, more rectangular stones as much as possible.

Building a wall of cut stones is almost a thing of the past. Professional stone-cutters are on the verge of extinction. Even the old-time handyman who had the knack of sizing up a stone, giving it a whack with a sledge and reducing it to the exact size and shape he wanted is disappearing. In other words, if you need to cut a few stones to fit hard-to-fill gaps in a wall, you probably won't find anyone who can do it for you or even show you how. You'll just have to hack away by yourself—probably with a cold chisel and hammer. In time you'll discover which stones have a definite grain and which do not, and you'll quit trying to make the latter conform to your wishes.

The stones available for a wall have a great deal to do with the width of the wall and the way it is built. If you're building a very low wall—say, one not more than 24 in. high—and have stones which break easily into rectangular blocks like oversized bricks, the wall can be made only a foot wide. But as the height of a wall increases and/or the stones become more irregular, the wall must be made wider. In fact, there are not many dry stone walls which are less than 18 in. wide; and there are thousands which range from 2 ft. upward.

Wall thickness also depends on your construction method. Some walls—the kind the new wall builder automatically sets out to erect —are only one tier thick; that is, the majority of stones extend all the way through the wall and are exposed on both sides. But if you have enough stones to work with, a two-tier wall is easier to build because the stones don't have to be balanced so carefully. In it, each side of the wall is independent of the other, and the space between is filled with rubble. The slight slant given to the sides helps to keep the wall from being knocked down by animals; the in-between space was popular with Yankee farmers because it gobbled up so many of the little stones that cluttered their fields.

The foundation for a dry stone wall is much less elaborate than that for a masonry wall. All you need is a trench about a foot deep

Dry stone walls on opposite sides of a narrow New England pasture. The wall in the foreground is over one hundred years old and has two tiers of rectangular stones. That in the background was built with whatever stones were turned up in the field. It is only one-tier thick but in some places is 5 ft. tall. It was built in the early 1700s.

Part of the strange beauty of an old dry stone wall is derived from the lichens that encrust the surface. At night, after a shower, they glow phosphorescent under approaching headlights.

in mild climates; 18 to 24 in. deep in cold climates. It should be about a foot wider than the wall. After tamping the bottom, fill the trench with small stones, gravel, and big stones that are too ugly or badly shaped for the wall itself. Pour these in with some care so that they form a stable base.

Stretch a pair of strings the length of the wall between tall stakes to mark the sides of the wall. They will help to keep the wall straight from end to end and from top to bottom (raise the strings as you raise the wall). They are not, however, meant to prevent you from projecting a few stones slightly out beyond them and recessing others behind them: some irregularity of the surfaces is a characteristic of all dry walls.

A slanting, or sawtooth, top course is typical of many Kentucky limestone walls. Originally the jagged edge was meant to dissuade livestock from leaping over the walls.

There is no set procedure for building a dry stone wall (as there is for building brick and concrete-block walls). You can work from the middle out, the ends in, or from one end to the other. Similarly, you can build up one section far ahead of another section. I've found, however, that I tend to work in logical order from end to end, and thus it's easier at the end of a day or week or month to gauge the progress I've made.

In laying stones, there are several things you should try to do and several you should try not to do.

1. Make sure that each stone is firmly set, so it doesn't wobble. If necessary, you can stick small shims or stone into the joints around a wobbler. But as a rule, the fewer shims you use, the more solid the wall.

2. In a two-tier wall, give each stone a slight downward slant toward the center of the wall so that, if it loosens, it will not fall out of the wall.

3. Try to place each stone so it overlaps two or more stones in the course below. Don't, in other words, pile one stone directly on another of the same size. The more the stones interlock, the stronger the wall.

4. Avoid the natural tendency to place stones so they all run lengthwise of the wall. Obviously, you should place the stones so their best faces are exposed. But if you have a long narrow stone that's as attractive at the ends as along the sides, set it at right angles to the face of the wall so you get some variation in the face.

5. Also avoid the tendency to use all your largest stones at the bottom of the wall so you won't have to lift them. It detracts from the appearance. Even without a burly assistant, you can hoist enormous stones to the top of a wall by skidding them up an inclined ramp of logs or by gradually building a crib of logs or 2×4s up under them.

Stone-masonry Walls   Using concrete to hold together a stone wall both simplifies and complicates the building process. But the end product has a more precise, formal look than a dry wall, and takes up less space.

I intend no disparagement of the appearance of stone-masonry walls. With exceptions, they're very handsome. In fact, because they are bound together with mortar, they can be patterned in more ways than a dry wall. You can, for instance, set plaques or unusual stones in the wall at definite intervals. You can mix bricks with stones as in the wall on pages 104-105. Or you can play tricks on the viewer by inserting in the wall stones which look like gargantuan boulders but which are in reality thin slabs set on edge.

But the real reason why masonry walls are built more often than dry walls is because they can be made much thinner yet taller, require less material, and generally last longer.

Because of the irregularities in the stones, most walls are at least 12 in. wide (which is 4 in. wider than a brick or concrete-block wall) and may be as much as 18 in. To hold them upright and prevent heaving, they must be built up from heavy footings about 1 ft. wider than the walls and 8 in. deep. These should be at least 18 in. below ground in frost-free climates; below the frost line elsewhere. (The measurement is made from the bottom of the footing to ground level.)

After digging the trench, line it on both sides with oiled boards to serve as forms. For a large wall, have the concrete brought in by truck and sluiced into the forms. For a small job, make your own mixture out of 1 sack Portland cement, 2¼ cu. ft. sand, and 4 cu. ft. coarse aggregate up to 1½ in. diameter. Strike the concrete off flush with the tops of the boards. Let the concrete harden for 24 hours before removing the forms and starting to build the wall.

Another way to make the footings is to toss unwanted stones into an unlined trench and to slush concrete down around them. If you own a rock pile, this saves some money; but it doesn't save much of any work because it takes time to surround the stones completely with mortar.

Build the wall to a pair of taut strings stretched between stakes. As in the case of a dry wall, if some of the stones project beyond or fall behind the strings a little, it doesn't detract from the wall. But don't stray from the lines too often.

The stones for the wall must be free of soil and other matter. Use a mortar made of 1 part Portland cement and 3 parts sand. The joints must be at least ½ in. wide, and many will inevitably exceed this. The first stones above the footing are embedded in mortar, just like all the others.

Put down mortar for only one stone at a time; and if possible, put more mortar on the end of the stone before setting it in place against the previously laid stone in the same course. (This is called buttering.) Because of the shape of some stones, however, this is not always possible; so after placing them in the horizontal mortar

A dry stone wall thick enough to defend a fortress. The bricks were deliberately mixed in with the limestone blocks for effect. The cap suggests a shed roof covered with wood shingles, because the top course overlaps the lower. All the cap joints are filled with mortar to improve water runoff. The tiles capping the gateway arch were specially made. PHOTO BY WARWICK ANDERSON

bed, you must trowel mortar into the joints around them until they are packed. In very large joints, if the mortar starts to sag, hold it in place with your hand. Finally, remove the excess mortar; finish the joints smooth and firm with your trowel or a piece of pipe; and wipe off any film of mortar left on the face of the stones with a damp rag. Generally, the less visible the joints, the prettier the wall. This doesn't mean, however, that you should make the joints so deep that there isn't enough mortar around the front edges of the stones to hold them.

Using mortar, you don't have to place stones as solidly as in a dry wall. But don't take chances. First set each stone in place without mortar. Even though it may wobble a little, if it stays put, it's a good fit. The mortar will anchor it. But if it insists on falling out of the wall when dry, it won't be very secure in mortar; so you should find another stone to take its place.

Most stones are laid lengthwise in a wall; but some fit better crosswise. These help to hold the two sides of the wall together. And as I said earlier, a few thin stones may be set on edge to make your friends ask, "How in the world did you ever lift that monster up on the wall?"

For a thick wall you may not have very many stones which extend all the way across the wall; so obviously you must lay two stones in parallel. Fill the void between them with mortar and small stones.

Use the best flat-sided stones you have to top the wall, and take care to work the mortar thoroughly into the joints so water won't trickle down into the wall, freeze, and open up a big crack.

Brick Walls   Brick is the most popular material for walls, and there's no doubt why it is: It's easy to lay—much easier than stone, because it is formed into neat rectangular cubes, and easier than concrete block because, although it takes roughly 16 bricks to fill the same space as one block, it weighs less. But the main reason why brick is the no. 1 choice is its beauty.

I don't think a brick wall is as beautiful as a New England or Pennsylvania stone wall, but it doesn't lag far behind. It has a gorgeous texture whether made of ordinary bricks or specially finished facing bricks. It seems to exude a delightful warmth (provided it isn't made of those nasty brownish-yellow bricks apartment-house builders favor). And it is a superlative background for plants.

(Top) *Brick wall around a swimming pool is built higher at the end where it's needed for privacy, steps down to pleasant sitting height elsewhere. It was built before the law called for a 4-ft. barrier completely encircling pools.* (Bottom) *Low brick wall with a thick flagstone cap sets a small garden area off from a rolling lawn to left of camera.*

A Massachusetts replica of
Jefferson's serpentine wall.
Erected to protect a property
against the noise of traffic
on two busy thoroughfares,
it had to be built higher at
a later date when it proved
to be only partly effective.
Rumor has it that the landscape architect who designed
the wall believed the undu-
lations would stop sound,
but they are totally valueless
in this respect. Recent ex-
periments prove that the
planting atop the wall negates its sound-stopping
ability to some extent
(see chapter 1).

More than that, you can create all sorts of interesting patterns by arranging the bricks in different ways and by making the mortar joints in different ways.

PLANNING A BRICK WALL   You can't just jump in and build a brick wall the way you build a stone wall. Since there are so many things it is possible to do, you must work out your plans first. Four points need to be considered:

Elaborate brick wall is topped with a brick cap shaped like a gable roof. Bricks in the inset panels are set in a common bond.

Wall dimensions: Brick walls are either one-tier thick (4 in.), two tiers (8 in.), or three tiers (12 in.) Practically all walls which are under 6 ft. high and are not exposed to strong wind pressure are two tiers thick. They require no reinforcement. If a wall is over 6 ft., however, or if it is over 4 ft. and exposed to strong wind, you should reinforce it with 16- $\times$ 16-in. brick piers spaced no more than 15 ft. apart. The alternative is to build a three-tier wall without reinforcement.

One-tier brick walls should not exceed 4 ft. and must be reinforced with 12- $\times$ 12-in. piers at 15-ft. intervals. However, you can omit piers if you build a serpentine wall like Thomas Jefferson's famed structure at the University of Virginia.

Brick sizes: There was a time when only three sizes of brick were available. Today, you can hardly count them. They range in thickness from a nominal 3 to 12 in.; in height from a nominal 2 to 8 in.; and in lengths up to a nominal 16 in.

Despite this wide selection, most people still stick to so-called standard bricks. These have nominal dimensions of $2\frac{2}{3} \times 4 \times 8$ in. Actual dimensions are $2\frac{1}{4} \times 3\frac{5}{8} \times 7\frac{5}{8}$ in. or $2\frac{1}{4} \times 3\frac{1}{2} \times 7\frac{1}{2}$ in. The former, or slightly larger, size is laid up with $\frac{3}{8}$-in. mortar joints; the latter, with $\frac{1}{2}$-in. joints.

There is no reason, of course, why you shouldn't use any other size you like; but generally the only advantage to be gained by this is a change in the appearance of the wall. Eight-inch jumbo bricks, however, can also save work.

Since nominal dimensions of the jumbos are $4 \times 8 \times 12$ in. (actual dimensions are $3\frac{1}{2} \times 7\frac{1}{2} \times 11\frac{1}{2}$ in. or $3\frac{5}{8} \times 7\frac{5}{8} \times 11\frac{5}{8}$ in.), it takes only two bricks to fill the space occupied by six standard bricks. This means you not only have less mortar to mix and apply but also have much less to do in actual lifting, placing, aligning, and setting of the bricks.

The only real drawback of the jumbos is that they are not finished as well on the back edge as on the face, so one side of a wall is not quite as attractive as the other.

Bonds: Some brick bonds have structural strength; others, known as pattern bonds, do not. For an unsupported wall in the garden, you should use a structural bond; if you use a pattern bond, tie the two faces of the wall together with short lengths of heavy galvanized wire bent into Zs. The ties are staggered and spaced not more than 2 ft. apart vertically and 3 ft. apart horizontally.

The most widely used structural bonds are:

Common or American bond in which five, six, or seven courses of bricks are laid lengthwise of the wall (these are called stretchers) and the next single course is laid crosswise (these bricks are headers). The vertical joints in the stretcher courses are staggered so that those in one course fall midway between those in the two adjacent courses.

In another type of common bond, the header course is composed of alternate headers and stretchers, as in a Flemish bond.

Flemish bond: Each course of bricks consists of alternate stretchers and headers, and the headers are centered on the stretchers in the courses immediately above and below.

English bond: This is composed of alternate courses of headers and stretchers. The headers are centered on the stretchers. The vertical joints in all header courses are aligned as are those in all stretcher courses.

Garden wall bond: A variation of the Flemish bond in which the headers in each course alternate with three stretchers. In a double-stretcher garden-wall bond, two stretchers rather than three are set between headers.

Popular pattern bonds are the running and stack bonds. The former consists entirely of stretchers laid so the vertical joints in one course are centered on the bricks in the adjacent courses. In the stack bond, the bricks are laid one directly over the other. Thus the wall is divided into a precise grid of horizontal and vertical lines.

Numerous other structural and pattern bonds can be created by such methods as increasing the number of header courses, increasing the number of stretchers between headers in the same course, installing soldier courses in which the bricks are laid vertically, laying bricks at a 45° angle as in a herringbone pattern, and projecting some of the bricks slightly beyond the face of the wall.

Mortar joints: The joints between bricks affect the appearance of a wall almost as much as the bricks themselves and the way they are arranged. Some joints are simply cut off, or struck, with a mason's trowel; others are shaped with special tools. The six in common use are:

Concave joint: A rounded joint made by tooling the mortar with a special tool or the end of a piece of pipe drawn along the joint.

V joint: A V-shaped joint made with a special tool or the corner of a board. Like the concave joint, it is very resistant to rain penetration if the mortar is firmly compacted.

Weathered joint: This joint is made with a mason's trowel angled backward and upward so that the top brick overhangs the joint a fraction of an inch. At the bottom, the mortar is flush with the edge of the brick below.

Struck joint: This is the reverse of a weathered joint and less watertight. The joint angles backward at the bottom.

Flush joint: In this the mortar is cut off flush with the faces of the surrounding bricks. It is the easiest joint to make but not always watertight.

Raked joint: A rectangular joint made with a special tool. The mortar is raked out to an even depth so the bricks above and below

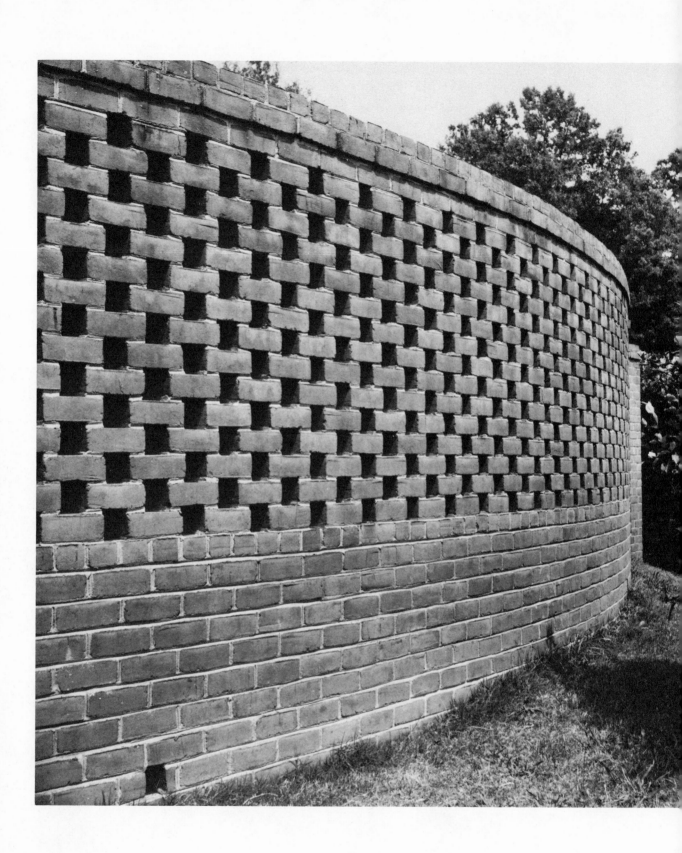

(Opposite) *A two-tier pierced brick wall serves as a windbreak and privacy screen around a swimming pool. (Top) The pierced panels in this wall are one-brick thick. The piers and wall below the panels are three-bricks thick. The lower part of the cap course is made of headers with joints raked out back to the panels. Because the wall was frequently scaled by youngsters, barbed wire was strung around the top on the back side. (Center) Heavy piers reinforce a semiopen brick wall and also break the wall at the points where it steps down a slight slope. (Bottom) Large openings add to the appearance of this wall and help drivers in the garage turnaround to see whether a car or pedestrian is entering the driveway. Yet the wall effectively screens the turnaround— rarely anything of beauty— from the street.*

project beyond it the same distance. It is not highly recommended for very wet or cold climates but produces a pronounced shadow line which increases the textured appearance of a wall.

A seventh kind of joint which does not require any tools is called the skintled joint. The mortar that squeezes out between the bricks is simply allowed to harden as it is. The effect is rough and sloppy but sometimes interesting.

BUILDING A BRICK WALL   Build the wall up from a concrete footing which is 18 in. below grade in frost-free areas, below frost line elsewhere. The footing should be 8 in. deep and 8 in. wider than the wall. Build it of concrete mixed to the same formula as that for a stone-masonry wall and poured into oiled forms.

A brick wall must be absolutely straight both horizontally and vertically. Because the sides are smooth and the mortar joints straight, the slightest deviation is obvious to the eye. To make sure the wall is true, stretch two strings taut between stakes at the ends of the wall before you start building; then, after you have laid up several courses, tie the strings around the ends of the wall itself. The strings help not only to keep the wall straight from end to end but also to keep the courses level. In other words, as you complete one course, raise the strings 2⅔ in. and use it to line up the next course.

To check further whether the wall is straight up and down, hold a carpenter's level against it from time to time.

Build the wall from both ends toward the middle. Until you reach the top of the wall, the ends are always two or three courses higher than the section in between. The tiers are built up together; that is, after you lay two or three bricks in the front tier, lay two or three in the back tier so the wall is the same height from front to back.

If you have never worked with bricks, you will find it takes a little practice to lay them perfectly; but since the first few courses above the footing are below ground, whatever mistakes you make will not be evident. By the time you are up to ground level, you will be an expert.

Wet the bricks thoroughly so they won't draw moisture out of the mortar. Soaking them for ten minutes in a tub of water is the best procedure.

For mortar, mix 1 part masonry cement (which contains a small percentage of lime) with 3 parts sand and enough water to make a plastic but not soupy mixture. If the temperature is over

114

80°, the mortar is usable for no more than 2½ hours after mixing; below 80°, it's usable for 3½ hours. If it dries out slightly during this period, retemper it by adding a little water.

Spread mortar on the wall for only two or three bricks at a time. For a stretcher course, put down a ribbon 4 in. wide and make a slight furrow down the center with the point of your trowel. For a header course, make the ribbon 8 in. wide and furrow it. The ribbons should be just thick enough so that when the bricks are pressed into them, they will form a joint ⅜ or ½ in. thick (depending on the dimensions of the bricks).

Before laying a brick, butter one end with a thick dab of mortar. Press the brick firmly into the horizontal ribbon and against the end of the brick previously laid. Be sure to set the brick squarely. Don't wiggle or slide it. Then tap it down with the handle of your trowel and scrape off the mortar which squeezes out in front.

The purpose of buttering the end of the brick is to assure a full vertical joint. Slushing mortar down into an open joint doesn't give the same result. Slushed joints are made only between tiers and at the ends of the closer, or final, brick laid at the middle of a course. Work the mortar down into the joints with the point of your trowel so all air pockets are eliminated.

Once you have spread a horizontal ribbon of mortar for two or three bricks, lay the bricks as fast as you can without making a poor job of it. The mortar must not dry out too much. If it begins to lose its wet glaze, scrape it up, mix it with the mortar in the mortar box, and start again.

If you place a brick incorrectly, don't try to straighten it because that weakens the bond with the mortar. Take it out, scrape up the mortar, replace it with fresh mortar, and reset the brick.

Finish the joints after the mortar has set a little. Wipe mortar stains off the bricks with a damp rag. Then, about two weeks later, scrub off whatever stains remain with a solution of muriatic acid (1 part acid in 9 parts water). Since the acid etches concrete, don't get any more of it into the joints than you can help.

Cut bricks as necessary by scoring them on opposite sides with a cold chisel. Then place the chisel on one of the lines and hit it with a hammer. Smooth the rough edges by rubbing them together.

If a wall turns a corner, build up both sides of the corner at the same time so they are firmly tied together by interlocking bricks at the apex.

To keep water from dripping into the wall and down its faces, top it off with a cap course or coping. Suitable materials include bricks laid across the wall on their narrow edges; flagstones, slates, or flat ledge rock; cast stone; and terra cotta.

In all cases, the cap should project at least ½ in. beyond the wall on both sides. All joints in the cap should be well offset from any cross joints in the wall.

Painting a brick wall can be done at any time after the mortar has set and cured for about a week. Use an exterior latex paint and

Wall of pierced concrete block separates a terrace on the far side from the neighboring property on this side.

apply it with a long-napped roller. Two coats are needed for full coverage. But don't be surprised if the paint doesn't perform as well as you hoped.

I hate to say this, because white-painted brick walls have a powerful appeal to me. But I have struggled with them unhappily for six years—and I see no respite in the future. Two things are wrong:

1. Some kinds of brick don't hold paint well in cold climates. Used bricks are the worst, but many new bricks are equally bad—though no one can tell which they are by looking at them. What seems to happen is that moisture gets into the bricks, freezes, and pops off the paint—sometimes with chips of the brick attached. But fortunately the problem is preventable at a small cost: Before applying the first coat of paint, cover the wall completely with a clear masonry sealer.

2. Green algae have an affinity for brick walls—especially in shady, damp locations. You can't see them when they first attach themselves; but suddenly they blossom out as a faint green film which in no time turns into a thick coating suggesting a moss. The algae grow on unpainted and painted walls alike; but since they are harder to see on the former, no one worries much about them. On painted walls, however, they are not only unsightly but also destructive to the paint. Within a year a newly painted wall must be painted again.

This is not to say that the algae are uncontrollable, because you can kill them by scrubbing with a strong solution of chlorine. This is essential when you repaint a wall. Even so, it is almost impossible to remove every speck of algae; so as soon as the new paint is applied, they go to work again.

Concrete-block Walls

Most of us think of concrete block as a drab, utilitarian material good only for building basement walls. But it makes an excellent, reasonably low-cost garden wall which need not be at all unattractive.

I admit that a wall built of standard 8- $\times$ 8- $\times$ 16-in. concrete blocks is not much to look at in its natural state; but given several coats of paint, it improves considerably.

Concrete-block walls really come into their own, however, when built with one of the many textured, sculptured, or pierced blocks which are available. If you want a wall of really modern design, here's the way to get it.

A unique fountain surrounded by a matching, vine-covered trellis beautifies a blank concrete block wall. The fountain is centered in the picture window facing the wall.

Since the great majority of concrete blocks are 8 in. thick, most walls are 8 in. thick. The height of a wall should not exceed 6 ft. unless it is reinforced at least every 15 ft. with 16- $\times$ 16-in. piers.

To avoid cutting blocks (which is done with a cold chisel), plan the wall so it is an exact multiple of the blocks' length. Drawing the wall to scale on paper not only will help you to visualize what you are building but also to order the exact number of blocks you will need. Your order list will include full-length stretchers with hollows in both ends; full-length corner blocks with one solid, flat end; half-length corner blocks with one solid end; and 4-in.-thick solid blocks to cap the wall.

Footings for a concrete-block wall are exactly like those for a brick wall. If your wall is to be solid and more than 4 ft. high, however, embed vertical ½-in. steel reinforcing rods in the footing while the concrete is soft. The rods should be long enough to extend from the center of the footing to 2 ft. above ground level. Install the first rod 16 in. from one end of the wall, and carefully space all others 4 ft. apart so they will project up through the cores of the blocks.

(Reinforcement is not required for a solid wall less than 4 ft. high or for a screen wall made of pierced concrete blocks.)

Blocks are laid from the ends of the wall toward the middle. Use a single string stretched between stakes to keep the wall straight when you start building; then fasten the string to the ends of the wall. But even with this as a guideline, you should check each block as you lay it with a carpenter's level to make sure it is both level and plumb.

For mortar, use 1 part masonry cement, 3 parts sand, and enough water to make a plastic mix. Make the joints ⅜ in. thick. Spread mortar for only one block at a time. On the footing, put down a strip the size of the block; but thereafter apply mortar only to the long front and back edges of the blocks in the course below. Do not cover the cross strips.

After applying the mortar bed, butter mortar on one end of the block you're about to lay; then press the block firmly into the bed and against the end of the block previously laid. Tap it firm, and scrape off the excess mortar. Tool the joint to a concave or V profile after the mortar has set somewhat.

As a rule, concrete-block walls are built with a running bond because the overlapping of the blocks in alternate courses adds to the strength of the wall. If you use a stack bond, tie the vertical rows of blocks to one another with galvanized hardware cloth or Z-shaped wires embedded in the horizontal joints.

If a wall is reinforced with steel bars inserted in the footing, pack concrete into the core spaces around each bar as you build up the wall.

Cap the wall with solid blocks laid flush with the wall faces.

Let the mortar dry for at least four or five days before painting the wall. You can then apply either Portland cement or exterior latex paint. One of the advantages of the former is that it becomes an integral part of the blocks and won't blister or peel. To apply it, sprinkle the wall with water; then scrub the paint into the pores with a fiber scrubbing brush; and as soon as the paint sets, give it a very fine water spray and keep it damp for 48 hours. Then apply a second coat in the same way.

Latex paint is much easier to apply and about as durable. Use a long-napped roller and put on two coats. If the block has a very rough, porous surface, however, use a thick block filler for the first coat.

BUILDING A SCREEN WALL   Pierced concrete blocks differ from standard blocks in that they have four flat, solid sides. They are therefore laid in a full mortar bed which extends from one side of the wall to the other.

Use a stack bond and secure each vertical row to the next with a tie of hardware cloth or Z-shaped wires. No reinforcing rods are used since wind can pass right through the wall.

The lowest exposed course of pierced blocks rests on standard blocks or poured concrete extending an inch or two above ground. A cap course of solid blocks is generally recommended to keep water out of the vertical joints in the wall, but it is sometimes omitted for sake of appearance. In the latter case, take pains to pack mortar solidly into the joints between the blocks in the top course.

Retaining Walls

Retaining walls must be built so they cannot overturn or slide forward. This presents a problem—often a difficult problem—since the weight of the soil and pressure of the ground water are substantial. Numerous walls have failed to meet the test or have been cracked from top to bottom.

Any wall over 3 ft. high (from ground level to the top of the wall) should be built by a professional. Poured concrete is the

Marking the outer edges of an informal entrance court for a modern house in rocky, wooded New England, this low wall is built of poured concrete capped with slate. The forms in which the concrete was poured were constructed (laboriously) to give the mortar the texture of old, rough boards of varying widths set in an irregular line.

The three types of poured concrete retaining wall. Left to right: a vertical-face gravity wall, backward-leaning gravity wall, and cantilever reinforced wall.

Ground Level

GRAVITY WALLS

CANTILEVER WALL

material usually used because it is far more resistant to cracking than brick, stone, or concrete-block masonry.

The three types of walls which are used are known as the vertical-face gravity wall, backward-leaning gravity wall, and cantilever reinforced wall. The choice depends on several factors including the soil, location, cost, suitability, and appearance. For instance, because a cantilever wall is relatively lightweight, it is generally the best on unstable soil. But both gravity walls are more resistant to sliding because of their greater weight. On the other hand, a backward-leaning gravity wall reduces the usable ground area at the top.

All three wall types are built up from a thick, wide footing laid below frost line or at least 18 in. deep in frost-free areas. In a cantilever wall, the wall and footings are tied together with reinforcing rods; but these are unnecessary in gravity walls. To assure

Poured concrete retaining wall topped with a lovely wood fence to keep people on the upper terrace from falling. Vines are trained on wires to soften the harsh appearance of the white concrete.

This is an incredible—and incredibly beautiful—California version of a Moorish water garden. It is surrounded by enormous poured concrete walls which in some areas hold back the hillside and in other areas tower above the land. Note the weepholes at the base.

(Top) *Big blocks of lime-stone laid without mortar in a retaining wall.* (Bottom) *A dry stone retaining wall of extraordinary height. It works because the stones are large and rectangular.* PHOTOS BY WAR-WICK ANDERSON

Concrete-block retaining wall has a slight backward slant to increase resistance to earth pressure. The wall is capped with a thin ribbon of concrete which has been given a slightly rounded contour to improve runoff of water. Even though half-size blocks are used on the curve, the courses above overhang them to produce an interesting shadow pattern.

drainage, a foot-thick layer of crushed rock is placed against the back of all walls; and 4-in.-diameter weepholes spaced about 10 ft. apart are provided in the walls above the footings. Additional weepholes above grade are also needed in high walls.

If a retaining wall is less than 3 ft. high, you can build it yourself; but observe the principles of constructing larger walls: Provide footings at least 12 in. wider than the wall. Give the wall as much mass as possible; otherwise tie it to the footings with reinforcing steel.

Construct poured concrete walls to one of the designs illustrated.

Concrete-block walls should be reinforced with steel rods embedded in the footing on 4-ft. centers. Fill the cores around the rods with concrete. Brick walls are similarly reinforced. The rods are inserted in the joint between the front and back tiers.

Stone retaining walls are built with or without mortar. In the latter case, use the largest stones you can handle, lay them up in a single tier, and make sure they are firmly set, using as few shims as possible. No weepholes are needed since water flows out through the joints.

An important step in building all retaining walls is to keep people from falling off them. Unfortunately, this is often ignored—especially in areas that are not frequently occupied. The best barrier obviously is a railing or fence built atop the wall or just behind it. But if this looks incongruous—as it may in an open yard or on a hillside which is supported by a series of retaining walls—plant low shrubs. An alternative is to put in a 2- or 3-ft.-wide flower bed or bed of groundcover just behind the top of the wall. This may not be an actual protection but serves as a warning to anyone who sees it or accidentally steps into it that he has strayed into an area where he is not wanted.

Wall Gardens

A wall garden is a kind of low retaining wall with flowers planted in the face. Built of stone, it not only prevents the ground behind it from sliding but also creates a delightful picture. Flowers and stones make a lovely combination.

Retaining wall of large, irregular concrete bricks. At the rear of the garden, a fence made of redwood grapestakes encloses a compost heap and work area.

(Top) *Low wall garden planted with perennials. The flowers were tucked into soil-filled joints as the wall was erected.* (Bottom) *This much higher wall garden is slanted backward 15° to 20° from the vertical in order to counteract the pressure of a very high, steep hill. Partly because of the slant, partly because the rocks are unusually flat, and partly because the soil is very porous, the wall shows no sign of giving way even after five years.*

Build the wall 2 ft. in front of the hillside and slope it backward 2 in. in every 1 ft. rise. Use flat stones 6 to 12 in. wide and slant them slightly downward toward the back of the wall.

Dig a trench somewhat wider than the wall and 6 to 12 in. deep and fill it with firmly packed gravel and small stones. As you build up from this, fill in behind the wall with good planting soil mixed with stones about the size of a baseball. Spread a thin layer of soil on the wall stones and in the joints between them, and lay the plants in this.

Spread the roots well. Set the plants so the crowns (the juncture of the roots and tops) are about 1 in. back from the wall face. Before placing the next course of stones, dampen the soil, and pour in plenty of water behind the wall. Plant additional flowers just behind the top of the wall. Mist the wall frequently with water until the plants take hold.

Any small perennial is suitable for a wall garden. Favorites include basket of gold, creeping phlox, sedum, thyme, violets, and armeria. Vines can also be used, but they will soon crowd out the flowers.

5 Gates

The gate is the focal point of every fence and wall. This is not just because people are looking for a way to get to the other side of the fence, but also because the gate serves as a visual break in the long and sometimes monotonous expanse to either side.

Our ancestors were especially appreciative of the value of gates because they went to considerable pains to make them beautiful. Some of their efforts are illustrated; and at first glance, you will probably say to yourself, "That's not for me. I don't have the time or know-how those old fellows did." But don't commit yourself too fast. Few of the gates are really difficult to build. (The finials on the gate posts are another matter: You would need a lathe for these or have to unearth them in a junkyard.) And if they are difficult, you might find or develop another design which is just as handsome and somewhat easier.

On the other hand, very simple gates can be beautiful, too. When I came on the two plain wooden gates shown below and on page 130, I knew instantly that I had to take pictures of them. I have seen many similar gates and passed them by without further notice. But somehow these were just right—in perfect keeping with their settings.

A simple but charming little gate made of 3-in. pickets nailed to a well-braced frame of 2 x 4s, and swung between 2 x 4 posts screwed to lead anchors in the stone-masonry wall.

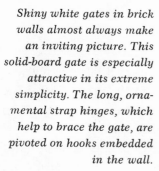

Shiny white gates in brick walls almost always make an inviting picture. This solid-board gate is especially attractive in its extreme simplicity. The long, ornamental strap hinges, which help to brace the gate, are pivoted on hooks embedded in the wall.

Planning a Gate

Five points must be decided before you start building a gate:

1. The design. This is a matter of choice. You can have a gate that is an exact or almost exact match of the fence. Or it can be—and in the case of a masonry wall must be—entirely different. In either case, the gate usually has a distinct front and back; and the front should face the same direction as the front of the fence.

2. The direction in which the gate will swing open. This depends on the location of the fence and location of the gate.

A beautiful wall, fence, and gate. Although the gate design is elaborate in the extreme, you could make one like it with a jigsaw.

If the fence is on your boundary line, the gate should swing open into your own property. This is not a hard-and-fast rule, but it's a good one to follow if there are not compelling reasons to the contrary, because you cannot be accused of trespassing on property that isn't yours. Furthermore, in a fence across the front of a property, an inswinging gate looks more welcoming; and if it is left open by mistake, some little boy is not so likely to come along and swing on it.

If the fence is within your property, these considerations are of little or no importance. Even so, there may be distinct advantages in choosing a frontward over a backward swing, or vice versa. For instance, if the preponderant flow of traffic is in one direction, the gate should probably swing in the same direction so it won't impede traffic. On the other hand, if the gate is located near one end of the fence, it is better for it to swing back—even against the traffic flow —toward the end of the fence so it will be out of the way when open. (This is similar to the way a door in the corner of a room is hung: It is always swung back into the corner so you don't have to walk around it to get through the door.)

3. The position of the gate relative to the front of the fence. This depends on the design of the gate, the direction in which it swings, and the size of the gate posts.

If the gate is designed like the fence, the face is usually flush with the face of the fence; and the gate must swing frontward. (If

(Right) *For a Victorian house a pair of identical Victorian gates.* (Opposite) *An entrance in the old Colonial manner. The fence and matching gate are made with round pickets inserted in the rails. Centered in a semicircular recess, the gate is slightly higher than the fence to add to its importance and to make it more in keeping with the scale of the gate posts which are, in turn, scaled to the three-story house. The entire structure is painted green like the shutters on the house.*

Such a graceful spindled gate is an uncommon center-piece for a dry stone wall. But it's effective, and that's what counts.

it were swung backward, the clearance on the latch side would have to be so wide as to be unattractive.)

If the gate and fence are of different designs, however, the gate can be either flush with the front of the fence or with the back side of the gate posts. If flush in front, the gate swings frontward; if flush in back, it swings backward.

If the gate and fence are of the same thickness, they are obviously in alignment on both the front and back and can swing in either direction. But if the gate posts are much thicker than the gate—as when a gate is set in a masonry wall—the gate is usually centered on the posts. It also can swing in either direction.

4. The position of the gate relative to steps. Actually, you have no choice here. A gate should always be placed at the top of steps—not at the bottom—so that a person approaching from the top will be warned of the steps and will not pitch down them. As an additional warning, the gate should swing away from the steps, thus forcing the pedestrian to come to a halt while he opens it.

134

(Top) *Massive boxed posts and handsome gate are a sharp contrast with the fragile-looking fence. The gate and fence are centered between the front and back sides of the posts, as is always the case when the posts are much thicker than they.* (Bottom) *A modern gate made of 2 x 4s in a chevron arrangement that is virtually immune to sagging. The timber posts are slightly tapered.*

(Top) Sturdy X-braced gate is made of boards the same width as the fence rails. The very slightly bowed top adds to the gate's charm. Without this, it would be rather ordinary. (Bottom) Unusual fence and gate are designed to give privacy from a busy street. Though passersby can't help noticing the gate, it has a definite keep-out look. Its only purpose is to provide access to the mailbox.

5. The slope of the walk or driveway. Since most gates are hung about 1 in. above walks and 2 or 3 in. above driveways, they have ample clearance to swing open if the ground is flat or has only a very slight slope. But if the paving has a definite lengthwise incline, this must be taken into account in the design or installation of a gate.

Happily, if a gate swings open downhill, so to speak, there is no problem: Provide the same clearance you would on flat ground. If a gate swings open uphill, however, you must either increase the clearance at the bottom or cut off the bottom of the gate to the same angle as the slope. The former solution is preferable. The latter should be used only when the bottom rail of the gate must, for appearance's sake, be aligned with the fence rail; and even in that case, the rail should be cut at such a slight angle that it is barely noticeable.

Narrow open joints in a plain board gate give a hint of what is behind. The gate would be improved if ornamental T hinges or almost concealed butt hinges had been used. The paint is flaking off the brick wall in places where algae have taken hold.

Building Gates I have no sage advice to offer about building iron gates except, "Don't try it." Wood gates, however, hold no terrors. The basic precepts about fence building apply to gates also.

Use sound, strong lumber. Strictly speaking, it need not be resistant to decay since it is not in direct contact with the ground. Nevertheless, because gates have numerous joints which moisture can enter, they are best built of redwood, cypress, or other wood treated with a preservative.

Use rust-resistant brass, aluminum, or galvanized-steel screws, nails, bolts, etc., to construct a gate. Because of the strains to which many gates are subjected, screws are preferable to nails for making most joints. If additional reinforcement of joints is advisable, use waterproof resorcinol glue.

Try to shape all horizontal surfaces so water will run off rapidly.

But the all-important point to bear in mind when designing and building a gate is that it must not sag or warp.

If a gate is made of vertical boards set edge to edge, two cleats fastened across the back about 6 in. down from the top and 6 in. up from the bottom usually provide all the stiffening and strength required. The cleats should be cut from 6-in.-wide boards and screwed to the face boards. Use at least two screws in each face board—one near the top of the cleat at the right side of the face board and one near the bottom at the left side of the face board. Add an additional screw in each end of the cleat.

On a high board gate such as that on the following page, a diagonal cleat should be added. Since the gate can sag only on the latch side (the hinges prevent sagging on the hinge side), the cleat should be installed between the top cleat on the hinge side and the bottom cleat on the latch side. (Use the same arrangement on all gates requiring diagonal bracing.)

All gates made with spaced pickets or slats must be diagonally braced; and a second diagonal brace that forms an X with the first is usually added. The latter, however, is installed mainly because an X looks better than a single diagonal; it has relatively little bracing strength because it is actually made in two pieces that fit on either side of the first diagonal.

Two-by-four timbers are required only in very large, heavy gates and in those with inset solid or open-work panels. In the case of large gates, the timbers are employed as cleats in the manner

138

This gate (adjacent to a matching carriage gate only partly shown) not only says keep-out but is actually so massive that it would take half of King Arthur's army to break through. Almost 8 ft. high, it's made of 2-in.-thick lumber held together by large, square-headed carriage bolts. The gate is dark brown; the hinge leaves, a medium-bright green.

Wishing to share the beauties of their walled garden, the owners of this old downtown Philadelphia home installed an iron gate so pedestrians could see through. But to gain privacy when the garden is the center of parties, they also installed an inner gate of solid boards—swung back against the wall.

*Towering wall separates
sections of one of the
country's most magnificent
private gardens, but the
arched gateway with its
handsome iron gate beckons
you from one garden area
to the other. A similar gate
elsewhere in the garden,
which is outside San
Francisco, drips with
fragrant wisteria blossoms.*

A similar gate and wall divide a garden outside Philadelphia.

This is the gate in the high board fence shown on page 15. Because it is solid, it is psychologically more of a deterrent to strangers than an openwork gate; but the lovely yard beyond seems to say, "Well, if you have legitimate business, enter." Note how the fence sections on either side of the gate overlap so that street noise passing around the end of the left section is stopped by the right section.

(Top) *A pergola with a double gate. Though old-fashioned, this is still a feature of many modern gardens.* PHOTO BY THE GENERAL ELECTRIC COMPANY (Bottom) *When you want a gate which gives maximum view of what is on the other side, steel is the first choice because even the slenderest members are extremely strong. This delicate looking structure is actually a double gate. A cane bolt locks the left section in closed position.*

just described; or they may be formed into a diagonally braced rectangle with boards, pickets, or slats nailed to the front.

When a gate has solid or openwork panels set into a frame of 2×4s, the bracing must be suited to the gate design. For example, if a solid, rectangular panel of plywood or acrylic is set into a frame, no bracing of any kind is called for since the panel itself prevents sagging and twisting of the frame. Similarly, if the inset forms an X within a 2×4 frame, it provides all the bracing necessary.

On the other hand, if an inset panel consists of horizontal bars or is formed like a plus sign, the frame must be braced in some way. If you know little about carpentry, ask a friend with more experience what he suggests. The simplest possibilities include mitering, rabbeting, or lapping the corner joints; screwing angle irons into the joints; reinforcing the joints with diagonal or concave wood blocks or boards; and bracing the entire gate with metal rods or wires stretched diagonally between corners.

Driveway and farm gates present still another problem because they are so wide that conventional bracing is inadequate to stop sagging. But two standard solutions have been in use for years.

The simpler is to hinge the gate to a post which is about twice as high as the gate; then extend a strong wire from the top of the post to the opposite top corner of the gate.

The other solution is to build the gate much higher on the hinge side than the latch side and run a diagonal board from the top of

146

This gate is similar to the preceding but it sags a little because the posts are lighter and are not attached to anything which pulls them away from the gate.

(Right, top) *Enormous farm gate is hinged to a massive granite post. A thick board running diagonally from the high hinge side of the gate to the opposite corner keeps gate from sagging.*
(Bottom) *This farm gate doesn't seem to lead anywhere now, but it must have been more important at one time to warrant the fancy design. Bracing is equally unusual. I suspect the diagonal brace to the right of the tall hinge post was added as an afterthought to hold the post—and gate—upright.*
(Opposite, top left) *Badly patched-up gate is held level by the stout steel cable from the top of the 8-ft. post to the upper corner of the gate on the latch side. Another cable running to the ground to right of the gate is needed to keep post from warping or snapping under the weight of the gate.*
(Right) *This enormous gate is not on the verge of collapse. It was hung this way so it would clear the sloping driveway when opened but would look normal when shut. The tilt could have been avoided if the gate swung open in the other direction, but that was impossible because it would have blocked the side-walk.*
(Bottom) *The curved diagonal is designed to prevent this driveway gate from sagging but is not completely effective. A third hinge should be added.*

the hinge side to the bottom corner of the latch side. Hang the gate on a high post with three or four large hinges. See the illustration on page 148.

Gate Posts

The ease with which a gate swings open and shut depends as much on the posts as on the gate itself. They must be absolutely straight and in line. If the gate, including cleats, is 1½ in. thick, space the posts to provide ½-in. clearance for the gate—⅛ in. on the hinge side, ⅜ in. on the latch side. But if the gate is thicker than 1½ in., the clearance on the latch side must be increased to ⅝ in.

Both posts are set in concrete (see chapter 3) at least 3 ft. deep. And for a very tall, wide, or heavy gate, the hinge post is sunk at least 4 ft. For a driveway or farm gate, the hinge posts should be further anchored by enlarging the posthole to 1-ft. diameter or more, and cramming the entire hole with concrete.

Four-by-four-inch timbers are adequate for all gate posts except those for driveway and farm gates. These should be 6 × 6 in.

In most cases, a gate is fastened directly to the hinge post with a pair of hinges located so they can be screwed into the horizontal

These stone gate posts in an old dry stone wall teach a lesson in gateway planning. They are 12 ft. apart, but because the driveway comes through at an angle, even trucks of moderate size have difficulty negotiating the passage; and stones in the post have been dislodged several times. Moral: The width of a gateway should be based not simply on the width of a moving van but also on the angle at which the van must enter.

Plant boxes give a nice finishing touch to gate posts.
PHOTO BY WARWICK
ANDERSON

cleats or frame of the gate as well as into the face panels. On small gates, 3- or 4-in.-high butt hinges like those used on the doors in your house are adequate. Mortise the leaves into the post and edge of the gate.

On large gates, T hinges are generally used. The rectangular leaf (corresponding to the crossbar of a T) is screwed to the gate post—either to the side of the post so it is hidden when the gate is closed or to the face of the post so it's exposed. In the latter case, the leaf is not set into a mortise. The triangular leaf is then screwed to the face of the gate without mortising. If you object to the appearance of the ordinary T hinge, ornamental designs are available. In the best of these, the triangular leaf, or strap, is very long and arrow-shaped.

Strap hinges, with two long triangular leaves, are sometimes used on very heavy gates that are flush with the gate posts (by contrast, butt and T hinges can be used whether a gate is flush with the posts or not). The leaves are screwed directly to the front

151

A gate not to be forgotten even though time has passed it by. PHOTO BY WARWICK ANDERSON

(Right) *Industrial gate made of aluminum is handsome enough for a residential property. (Opposite) An old farm gate built for easy, frequent operation. The top rail pivots on a pipe driven into the top of the hinge post and extends far to the side. At the end is a wooden cradle filled with rocks to counterbalance the gate. Thus the gate remains level when open. The wire across the top which braces the gate is unusual.*

Gateway to the parking area just in front of a country home behind the camera. The huge urns mark the gateway's location for cars coming down the curving drive.

of the gate and post without mortising. If the leaf attached to the post is longer than the post is wide, bend the end around the post.

A fourth type of hinge which may be used for hanging gates of all sizes and designs is a combination screw hook and strap hinge like that for hanging shutters. The L-shaped hook is screwed into the center of a gate post; the hinge, attached to either side of the gate, slips over it. The principal advantage of the unit is that it permits ready removal of the gate whenever that gets in the way or needs scrubbing or painting. In addition, if the hooks are allowed to project far enough from a gate post, the gate can be swung open in both directions. On the other hand, even when the hooks are screwed all the way into a post, there is a gap of at least ¼ in. between the gate and post.

Gate posts, of course, are not always 4- × 4- or 6- × 6-in. exposed timbers. In many formal fences, they are made of 8- or 10-in.-wide boards nailed together to form a square pillar; while in walls, they may be 12- or 16-in.-square piers. In both cases, gates

156

are hung on the center lines of the posts; that is, midway between the front and back edges.

The core of a boxed board post is a solid timber which is sunk in concrete as previously described. The boards are nailed to the timber. Screws used to mount the hinges on the post must be long enough to penetrate through the boards about 1 in. into the timber; otherwise the weight of the gate will eventually rip them loose.

Hanging a gate on a masonry post or wall is usually done with combination screw hooks and strap hinges. Ideally, these should be installed while the hinge post or wall is being constructed so that hooks with flat rather than threaded shanks can be inserted in the mortar joints. If installation is delayed until the post is completed, you must bore holes in the post or wall with a carbide-tipped drill; set in lead anchors; and screw the hooks into these.

The only other way to hang a gate on masonry is to fasten a 2×4 vertically to the side of the post or wall with screws driven into lead anchors; and then to fasten the gate to the 2×4 with butt or T hinges. Thus the width of the gate is several inches less than the space between gate posts. This is a possible minor disadvantage of the installation which is not offset by any appreciable advantages. Nevertheless, there are some instances when this method of installation is preferable. For example, the operating part of the gate illustrated on page 158 is hung in this way so it will clear the brick coping on the wall. Similarly, the gate on page 129 is hung in this way because it can be fastened more securely to the rough stone walls than might be possible with screw hooks.

Semicircular gateway says, "Welcome to Green Shadows." From the board fence just visible at left, the wings of the gateway build up gradually to the tall central posts.

(Top) *This gate was built almost 15 ft. wide in anticipation of the time when it would have to be used by trucks and bulldozers to construct a swimming pool on the other side. Since the pool was completed, the big right section has been anchored by a 2 x 4 at the left end; but it can still be opened when bolts holding the 2 x 4 are removed. The top is slightly bowed to improve the gate's appearance.* (Bottom) *A farm gate attractive in its simplicity. Because it is rarely used and is supposed to be kept closed, no attempt has been made to prevent sagging when open. In fact, the only thing that stops sagging when the gate is closed is the hasp.*

Completing a Gate Installation

Once you've hung a gate and tested its swing, install a stop on the latch post to prevent the gate from swinging past the post when closed. The stop is nothing more than a narrow board ($\frac{1}{2} \times 1$ in., 1×1 in., 1×2 in., etc.) cut to the height of the gate. To install it, close the gate and draw a pencil line along its back edge on the latch post. Then nail the stop to this line with finishing nails.

Next to the common hook-and-eye, the most widely used gate latch is the old-fashioned thumb latch in which the tongue is raised by a thumb depresser on one side of the gate and by an L-shaped handle on the other side. This is the most attractive of the latches available in hardware and building supplies stores.

Self-latching latches are strictly utilitarian but have a more positive action than thumb latches. You can close and latch a gate simply by giving it a push. To open it, you flick a trigger. Although the latch is mounted entirely on the back of a gate, it can be operated just as easily from the front. A padlock can be inserted for complete security.

Another useful latch is a spring-actuated unit which is screwed to the top of a gate. It is opened by pressing a trigger with your thumb; latches automatically when the tongue slides over the strikeplate. It is sold with two strikeplates—one which is mounted on the top of the gatepost flush with the latch; the other which is mounted on the side of the post.

Hasps and sliding bolts may also be used. But both must be opened and closed manually; and if a gate has even a slight sag, they can be operated only if you put a toe under the gate and raise it until the two parts of the latch are in alignment.

Although generally not needed, a spring can be installed to close a gate after people have walked through. The kind used is a heavy wire coil which is mounted diagonally across the gap between the gate and hinge post and works like an ordinary screen-door spring. But unfortunately, because the coil rests on the back of the gate and post, it wears a groove in both after the gate has been opened repeatedly.

To hold a gate open or to hold it secure when locked, mount a cane bolt on the back at the bottom latch-side corner. The bolt is a $\frac{1}{2}$-in. L-shaped steel rod which slides up and down in a pair of brackets. The point at the bottom slips into a hole drilled in the paving under the closed gate or into a pipe hammered into the ground under the open gate.

(Top) Thumb latch. (Bottom) A self-latching latch. When the gate is pushed shut, the rounded section automatically pushes up over the strike (which is a projecting steel rod). To open the latch, push the trigger on top or pull the weighted cord running through the gate.

159

Gateways   Many gates are simply openings in a fence or wall; but they need be no less attractive than swinging gates. How you treat them depends on the importance you give them.

In my well-walled property, I have no less than nine open gates or gateways. Six are just gaps in the stone walls and fences. They are more or less hidden or unused, so there is no reason to make a feature of them. Nevertheless, most are quite charming. The ends of the walls on either side are carefully squared and finished. Only two might be improved. These are in fences, and they lead me to the conclusion that simple gaps in fences don't have the same quality as gaps in walls. They tend to look more like accidents than gateways.

My three other gateways are more elaborate because they are more important. They're meant to call attention to themselves. One is at the mouth of the driveway; another points the way to the swimming pool at the end of the lawn; and the third is between the flower garden and lawn. All three are flanked by gate posts higher than the adjacent stone walls or fences; and the frames thus created give greater emphasis to the openings in between (just as a frame focuses attention on a painting).

In a wood fence, the posts for a gateway are almost always made by boxing in a timber sunk 3 ft. in the ground (but not necessarily encased in concrete). At the top, the posts have wide overhanging caps with cornice moldings under the edges. In the old days, finials were set on top. The overall height of the posts is roughly 10 to 50 percent greater than the fence height; but occasionally it is even more.

In a wall, the gate posts are piers 4 to 8 or perhaps even 12 in. wider than the wall. The height rarely is more than half again that of the wall, and usually is less. The overhanging caps may be topped with ornaments such as concrete balls or urns; but while these were popular in the past, they seem too ostentatious for today. I much prefer tubs of flowers—as long as they are kept in good array.

Stiles   My guess—and it is only that: I have done no research—is that stiles were originated by farmers who had to keep their livestock from straying but wanted an easy way to get "through" the walls themselves. So instead of putting in gates, which would need

A turnstile lets people through but stops bicycles, tractors, lawnmowers, and other machines.

Stile over a country wall.

mending, they built stone steps up one side of the wall and down the other.

Few Americans today have livestock—only dogs that can negotiate steps as well as a human; consequently we haven't much use for stiles. Yet there's a place for them in some situations.

One of my neighbors built a stile several years ago. He lives at the intersection of a country highway and side road. The entrance to his house is off the side road, but his mailbox is on the highway. So rather than putting a gate in the wall along the highway, thus encouraging deliverymen and strangers to traipse to the front door by the wrong route, he built a stile to provide access to the mailbox. I see him every once in a while going over it. He looks a little like one of my Pilgrim ancestors. But what's wrong with that? They came up with some dandy ideas.

6 Espaliers and Fence Plantings

In their catalogs, many nurserymen give enticing descriptions of "living fences"; but they are just indulging in a play on words. Looking at the pictures, you will discover at once that the living fences are nothing but hedges—and hedges are outside the scope of this book.

But there is a kind of living fence which isn't a hedge and therefore merits discussion here. It's properly called an espalier.

An espalier is a woody plant trained on a vertical trellis to form a decorative, two-dimensional screen. As a rule, the screen is placed a few inches in front of a solid wood fence, masonry wall or any kind of house wall; but occasionally it is set far away from all such structures and thus becomes a fence in its own right.

A mighty pretty one it is.

Building the Trellis

Building a trellis for espaliering plants looks like such an easy task that the natural tendency is to slight it. The work is easy enough; but the trellis will look messy if you don't take time over it.

Minimum height of the trellis is 4 ft., and 6 ft. is about maximum for easy maintenance of the plants. Note, however, that if you want a much higher fence, there probably isn't anything in your city building code that prohibits it because hedges and living fences are not considered to be in the same category as conventional fences and walls.

Use 6- × 6-in. square timbers or 6-in. rounds for the two end posts; 4 × 4s in between. Space the posts 8 to 10 ft. apart. Set those at the ends at least 3 ft. into the ground and surround them with concrete. Sink the intermediate posts 2 to 3 ft. and omit the concrete.

The wires strung between the posts should be no. 9 galvanized steel. Install the top wire 2 to 3 in. below the tops of the posts, and space the other strands 1 ft. apart. At the ends of the fence, attach the wires to galvanized steel eyebolts driven through the posts. At the intermediate posts, simply run the wires loosely through ½-in. holes drilled in the posts. Pull the wires as taut as possible. It will help if you use a fence stretcher. Retighten them every year thereafter.

Espaliered apple trees form a delightful living fence around a parking area. In spring the fence is bright with white blossoms. In the fall it is laden with delicious fruit.

(Top) Whether these two small trees should be called espaliers is debatable, but at least the owner is trying to train them on the fence, and in an odd way, he has succeeded pretty well. But the really decorative feature of the fence is the shadow cast by the overhanging tree. (Bottom) Vines on trellises break the lines of an almost over-powering white-painted brick wall across one side of an entrance court.

(Top) Wood trellises are provided for climbing roses on this spaced board wall. They would look better if they matched. (Bottom) This picket fence is set atop a low brick wall and between brick piers. English ivy is allowed to climb on the brick but is carefully kept off the wood. The fence is unusual in that its back faces the street. But the decision to build in this way was wise because the horizontal lines of the rails, contrasting with the ivy-covered posts, add to the attractiveness of the fence.

Planting and Training
Espaliers

To the purist gardener, an espalier is a fruit tree. But most gardeners now call any tree or shrub that is trained to a two-dimensional design an espalier. As a result, the list of plants which are especially suitable for espaliering includes fruits and nonfruits, evergreens as well as deciduous plants:

Apple	Magnolia, southern
Apricot	Mock orange
Bottle brush	Peach
Cherry	Pear
Crabapple	Plum
Currant	Podocarpus
Firethorn	Quince
Flowering quince	Stewartia
Gooseberry	Tamarisk
Holly, Japanese	Yew

Select the plant you like best and stick to it from one end of the fence to the other. This does not mean, however, that you must stick to a single variety of fruit. On the contrary, if you plant apples, sweet cherries, plums, or pears, you must plant two or more varieties in order to have a bountiful harvest every year.

The actual plants used for espaliering are just like those grown in the normal way. Just be sure to start with small, young plants—not those that have grown old enough to be somewhat set in their ways. Buy them from a well recommended nursery, because it doesn't pay to put a lot of work into poor specimens which may not survive. And select dwarf varieties of all tree fruits except apricots and peaches.

Many people buy plants which are already trained as espaliers. This, of course, saves them several years of work but doubles or triples their initial expense. It also means that they must be content with the pattern in which the plants have been started.

If you train your own espaliers from the outset, you can follow any pattern you like. A number of these, such as the palmette verrier, cordon, Belgian fence, and candelabra, are formal patterns which have been used by European gardeners for several centuries. But there's no reason why you shouldn't create your own pattern as long as you carry it through to completion. After all, an espalier isn't

Chippendale-design fence serves as background for the fine perennial border on the far side and also marks the dividing line between the lawn area and cutting and vegetable garden (unseen to left).

The varied textures of lush tropical plants vie with the texture of a pierced concrete-block wall.

like a piece of needlepoint: Once it has been well started in a certain design, you can't retrain it in another design.

Plant the trees or shrubs directly under the wires of your trellis. How much space you provide between them depends on the form in which you will train them. For instance, trees are planted only 2 ft. apart in a Belgian fence whereas they should be 8 to 10 ft. apart in a double horizontal cordon.

If you plant open-foliaged shrubs and trees in front of a light-colored wall or fence, you can't help creating a pretty picture. The effect is accentuated here because the wall is bathed with white light directed upward from floodlamps in the ground at the base of the wall. PHOTO BY JOHN WATSON

If you plant in early spring (usually the best time, although fall planting is permissible), trees or shrubs will start making growth in a few weeks. From that time on, for the next several years, you will have to watch and fuss over them often to see that they develop as they should. The work is a great deal more pleasureable than difficult.

Major, basic pruning should always be done in early spring when the plants are dormant. But succulent new growths which you don't want can and should be removed at any time throughout the growing season because the whole idea of an espalier is to create a fence with a distinct, open pattern—not to let it become so choked with twigs, leaves, flowers, and fruits that it is an amorphous mass.

Training is done when the branches are young and supple. Select those that are growing out to the sides (more or less parallel with the trellis) at the desired height and in the desired direction,

172

(Top) Ancient, wind-torn tree is silhouetted against a tall pierced brick wall which separates the parking area from terrace (and also helps to support the openwork roof of the terrace). The tree is planted with succulents which are here being water-misted from concealed nozzles and tubes.   (Bottom) To soften the appearance of this very high, blindingly white concrete wall and make it look lower, raised planting beds were put in along the base and filled with shrubs and flowers. In several places, seagrapes are planted in front of the wall to display their angular trunks, multi-colored bark, and huge leathery leaves.

(Top) Andromedas massed on either side help to focus attention on the steps leading up through this stone-masonry retaining wall. (Bottom) To avoid the boxy, confined look that characterizes most city gardens, Boston landscape architect Stanley Underhill started by building a graceful redwood screen to hide a tool shed and parking space at the rear of the garden. The screen, made of narrow, spaced boards, makes an arc matching the bowed windows of the house. Then Underhill planted evergreens at the base of the screen in a border that curves another way, and he paved the garden in small granite blocks arranged in an intricate pattern of small overlapping fans. The fences at the sides of the garden are made of boards and alternating panels of large wood half-rounds.

and tie them to the wires at 8- to 12-in. intervals with soft, strong twine or strips of cloth. Cut out all other branches and rub off the twigs and buds you don't want on the tied branches.

When tying branches, take care not to pull the twine through the bark; and remember to remove it entirely—or replace it with a looser tie—after the branches have become established in the right positions.

Don't try to bend branches all at once to a sharp angle. Proceed gradually—a little this week, a little more next.

When your plants finally attain their correct size and shape, there is little if any additional training to do. But you must continue pruning on a regular basis to remove buds that would otherwise develop into new shoots and branches. Also to limit growth, give the plants no more fertilizer than they absolutely need to stay healthy and fruitful. As long as you start them out in good soil and work more humus into the soil every year, they will have ample vigor and require very little additional nutriment.

Planting To Beautify Other Fences and Walls

As I've said before—several times—nothing brings out the full beauty of plants as much as a masonry or solid wood background; and nothing does as much as plants to soften the lines, relieve the monotony, or reduce the apparent height of a solid wood fence or masonry wall.

This doesn't mean that when you build a fence or wall you should array plants against it from end to end—unless it is made of chain-link. That negates much of the value of your construction. A few plants carefully placed give an infinitely better effect.

Neither does it mean that you must actually place the plants close to a fence or wall—although here I get some argument. My wife and I, for instance, disagree about one of the high white brick walls around our home. There are some low shrubs at the base and a conical evergreen at one end; but she thinks the wall looks barren and needs a tall espalier or trained vine near the other end. I contend, however, that the moving shadows cast on the wall by a nearby sycamore do even more to relieve and add interest to the blank area. I have a great liking for shadow patterns.

When I say that fences need planting and plants enjoy fences, I mean no more than that. They go together perfectly, so they should be planned together.

The planning starts with your consideration of four points:

175

1. If a fence or wall is painted or stained, you should not put in vines that will cling to it because you won't be able to refinish it properly without tearing off the plants and scraping off the little tentacles and rootlets that are left sticking to the surface. That's a chore. Even worse, you probably won't be able to retrain the plants on the fence. Instead, you'll have to cut off the old shoots and wait for new ones to grow back in their place.

In other words, if plants are trained on a painted or stained barrier, they should be of the type that grows by twining or by means of tendrils, or that you tie in place. For the twiners and tendril-climbers, stretch wires or wire mesh on the fence. Those trained by hand are simply tied to nails or other anchors driven into the fence.

2. Use clinging vines only on unpainted walls. But remember that most of these form dense mats close to the surface; consequently, the surface is slow to dry out after storms and this gradually weakens mortar joints which have not been properly made (see chapter 4).

Growing clinging plants on unpainted fences is inadvisable because they precipitate decay. If you insist on using them anyway, treat the entire fence with wood preservative.

3. Avoid growing wisteria, bittersweet, climbing roses, and similar extremely vigorous vines on light-weight fences, such as those made of latticework, because the fences may collapse under their weight or literally be ripped apart by the stems working into the joints. Of course, such calamities can be prevented by regular pruning of the vines; but during the course of a busy summer there are so many other things to do that it's easy to forget this little chore.

4. If you or your neighbors have ever had trouble with green algae growing on any kind of exterior structural surface, there is a good chance you will have the same problem with a new fence or wall. To reduce the odds, don't train vines on the fence. Plant shrubs in front of it instead; and provide as much space as possible behind them so that the light and air, which discourage algae growth, can reach the fence.

Above all, don't paint the fence, because algae will destroy the paint and increase the difficulty of repainting.

ESPALIERS There is disagreement among expert gardeners about how espaliers should be grown against a fence or wall. Some insist that a wire trellis similar to that used for a free-standing espalier should be constructed 6 in. out from the fence so air can circulate around the plants. (The wires can be attached either to posts driven into the ground or to large lag screws projecting from the fence.) Others maintain that the trellis can be omitted—in which case, the plants are tied to nails driven into the fence.

In this garden the brick walls were built both to create flat spaces on a hillside and to define the several areas into which the garden is divided. Dark green Japanese hollies and boxwoods are planted on either side of the walls to soften their stiff horizontal lines.

I have seen no firm evidence that one method produces better or worse espaliers than the other. But in the long run, the trellis method saves work because, even though the trellis itself takes time to build, it makes for easier maintenance of the fence or wall behind the espaliers. In addition, the chances of getting algae on the fence are reduced by the 6-in. air gap. On the other hand, if you're training a single espalier on a fence, the effect will be much better if the plant is fastened to the fence rather than to an unsightly network of wires.

Regardless of whether a trellis is used, the plants are pruned and trained in the way described earlier.

VINES AND CLIMBERS   One advantage of clinging vines such as English ivy, climbing hydrangea, and wintercreeper is that, once you have planted them in front of a wall, they will climb it without assistance. All you have to do is keep them headed in the right direction.

177

If you want to blanket a fence or wall with vines which climb by twining (for example, wisteria or akebia) or by putting out tendrils (for example, ampelopsis or clematis), cover the surface with chicken wire nailed to cleats of 1-in.-thick wood strips. Thus the vines can weave their way through the mesh and can be taken down with the wire when the fence needs repainting. The alternative is to run a single long strand of aluminum wire through screw eyes in a zig-zag or grid pattern. But this arrangement cannot be removed for painting.

Twining and tendril vines can also be trained on a wood lattice. This creates an attractive design on a blank fence or wall even though the vines do not entirely cover the lattice. On the other hand, the lattice itself must be painted to keep it looking neat; and in order to do this, you must strip off the vines.

To train vines in a definite pattern on a fence or wall, arrange single wires on the fence in the desired pattern. Use screweyes or eyebolts to hold them out from the surface. The vines will follow the wires as naturally as a hunting dog follows a scent; and if occasionally it wanders off course, you can guide it back by hand.

SHRUBS   Shrubs and small trees planted at the base of a fence or wall are less troublesome than vines and espaliers because they require only occasional pruning; and when the fence needs painting, you can pull them away from it with ropes or canvas drop cloths so you can paint behind them.

In addition, you have a much wider choice of plants to work with and can create more of a three-dimensional effect than is possible with vines. The best species to use are those with distinct shapes which stand out in bold relief against the fence. Small conical and columnar evergreens are especially attractive. But my favorites are plants with lacy foliage or stems that form an interesting, irregular pattern. Japanese maples, for example, are outstanding because they have gorgeous feathery foliage and branches which form entrancing silhouettes. Other excellent plants are bamboos, heavenly bamboo (nandina), euonymus alatus, crape myrtles and seagrapes (though both grow taller than most fences), and tamarisks.

Index